P9-CEK-273

THE LINDBERGH BABY KIDNAPPING IN AMERICAN HISTORY

Other titles *in American History*

IN
AMERICAN
HISTORY

THE LINDBERGH BABY KIDNAPPING IN AMERICAN HISTORY

Judith Edwards

Enslow Publishers, Inc.

40 Industrial Road   PO Box 38
Box 398   Aldershot
Berkeley Heights, NJ 07922   Hants GU12 6BP
USA   UK

http://www.enslow.com

Library of Congress Cataloging-in-Publication Data

Edwards, Judith, 1940–
    The Lindbergh baby kidnapping in American history / Judith Edwards.
        p.   cm. — (In American history)
    Includes bibliographical references and index.
    Summary: Examines the famous kidnapping of aviator Charles
Lindbergh's baby, describing the background of the boy's father, the
circumstances of the crime, and the capture and trial of the alleged
kidnapper.
    ISBN 0-7660-1299-9
    1. Lindbergh, Charles Augustus, 1930–1932—Kidnapping, 1932
Juvenile literature. 2. Kidnapping—New Jersey—Hopewell Juvenile
literature. 3. Trials (Kidnapping)—New Jersey Juvenile literature.
4. Lindbergh, Charles A. (Charles Augustus), 1902–1974 Juvenile
literature. 5. Hauptmann, Bruno Richard, 1899–1936 Juvenile literature.
[1. Lindbergh, Charles Augustus, 1930–1932—Kidnapping, 1932.
2. Lindbergh, Charles A. (Charles Augustus), 1902–1974. 3. Hauptmann,
Bruno Richard, 1899–1936. 4. Kidnapping.] I. Title. II. Series.
HV6603.L5E38   2000
364.15'4'0974965—dc21   99-30815
                                                        CIP

Printed in the United States of America

10 9 8 7 6 5 4 3 2 1

To Our Readers:
All Internet addresses in this book were active and appropriate when
we went to press. Any comments or suggestions can be sent by e-mail to
Comments@enslow.com or to the address on the back cover.

Illustration Credits: AP/Wide World Photos, p. 25; Enslow Publishers,
Inc., p. 12; Judith Edwards, pp. 35, 38, 87, 116, 117; Library of
Congress, p. 47; New Jersey State Police Museum, pp. 8, 10, 13, 15, 21,
29, 33, 44, 55, 60, 65, 66, 69, 72, 81, 91, 95, 100, 110, 115.

Cover Illustration: New Jersey State Police Museum (Large center
photograph—the first ransom note); AP/Wide World Photos.

★ Contents ★

A FAMOUS BABY DISAPPEARS

The first of March was a cold and blustery evening, not even hinting at spring to come. Because the bouncy, blue-eyed baby with the yellow curls had a bad cold, his mother and nursemaid dressed him warmly. A flannel shirt, quickly sewn up by nurse Betty Gow, was put on little twenty-month-old Charlie before he was tucked in between warm blankets. Safety pins attached the blankets to the mattress to make sure he would not wriggle out of his covers on this chilly evening in 1932. The window was left a little ajar for fresh air.

After making sure the baby was falling asleep, Betty Gow turned off the light and left the room. She checked on him again around 7:50 P.M., and then went to the living room to tell Charlie's mother, Anne, that he was asleep. Anne Morrow Lindbergh was writing at her desk and waiting for Charlie's father to come home.

On March 1, 1932, little Charlie was the most famous baby in America. His father, Charles A. Lindbergh, had been the first man to fly nonstop across the Atlantic Ocean alone. For this reason, Lindbergh was often called the Lone Eagle, or Lucky Lindy, by people all over the world. Lindbergh was a hero. Little Charlie, Charles and Anne Morrow Lindbergh's first son, was nicknamed the Eaglet or Baby Lindy.

When Charles Lindbergh came home that night, he and Anne ate dinner and then got ready for bed. Betty Gow went in to check on the baby at about 10:00 P.M. When she went to the crib, she became alarmed that she did not hear little Charlie breathing. She bent down to pick him up and found that, although the blankets and pillow were still there, Baby

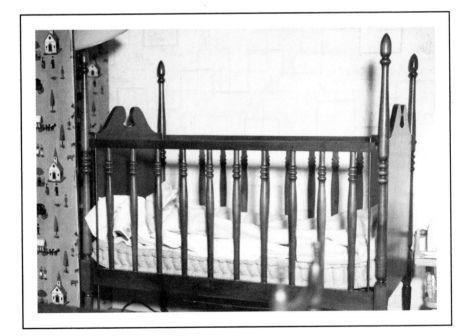

Betty Gow checked the Lindbergh baby's crib to find him missing, but the blankets still in place.

Lindy was not! Gow became very frightened and went to Mrs. Lindbergh, asking if she had the baby with her. Anne thought he might be with his father.

Gow ran downstairs and said, "Colonel Lindbergh, do you have the baby? Please don't fool me."

"No, of course not," answered Charles Lindbergh. "Isn't he in his crib?"

Becoming more and more upset, Gow said, "You must have the baby, he's gone."

Charles and Anne Lindbergh and Gow ran into the nursery. The baby was not in his crib or anywhere in the room. Turning to his wife, Charles Lindbergh said, "Anne, they've stolen our baby!"[1]

This terrible discovery was the beginning of a kidnapping case that would occupy the minds and imaginations of all America—and most of the rest of the world—for the next four years. The absolute fact that Charles Lindbergh, Jr., had disappeared was just about the only absolute fact that could be proven in those four years.

The confusion and frenzy began that night of March 1, 1932, when the Lindberghs' butler called the local police station in the little village of Hopewell, New Jersey. Except for the Lindberghs' new estate, the phones in town were at small farms and businesses. Most were party lines, where more than one person shared a phone number. When the unlisted number, HO (for Hopewell) 303 rang, it woke the night switchboard operator. It was obviously from Sorrel Hill, the new Lindbergh estate located on 360 acres at the foot of Sourland Mountain. The operator put the call through to the police. Constable Charles W. Williamson answered. The calm voice of the English butler said, "Colonel Lindbergh's son has been stolen. Will you please come at once."[2]

Even before the Lindberghs moved to Sorrel Hill, the people living in Hopewell knew exactly where the mansion was, and who owned it. Charles Lindbergh was America's biggest hero. Soon after the call to the Hopewell police, the whole town knew what had happened. By later that night, it would seem as if all nine hundred inhabitants had climbed the steep road to Sorrel Hill to investigate the situation for themselves.

The Lindbergh estate at Sorrel Hill as it looked at the time of the kidnapping.

Lindbergh himself called the New Jersey State Police and told Detective Lewis Bornmann that his son had just been kidnapped, sometime in the evening between seven-thirty and ten o'clock. He described what Charlie had been wearing—a one-piece sleeping suit and a flannel undershirt—and said that the baby was twenty months old.

The first to arrive at the estate, about 10:35 P.M., were Constable Williamson and the Hopewell police chief, Harry H. Wolfe. Charles Lindbergh was waiting at the doorway of the two-and-a-half-story white house. He was holding a rifle. Lindbergh took the officers outside the house, beneath the nursery windows. It was very muddy, and they walked on wooden planks that had been put down by carpenters who had been working on the house that day. On the ground, about seventy-five feet away from the window, they found part of a ladder. Near it were two more wooden ladder sections. A dowel pin—used to hold the ladder together, and a chisel—a tool used to shape wood, were nearby. They also saw marks under one of the nursery windows that could have been made by the legs of a ladder, and footprints pointing southwest.

Then Lindbergh took the policemen inside his home and led them to the nursery. There, they inspected the room. Lindbergh pointed out an envelope that was lying on a windowsill. It must have been left by the kidnappers, he said. He had waited to open it until the police arrived. The envelope had no writing on it, and it was sealed. When Corporal Joseph Wolf, a state

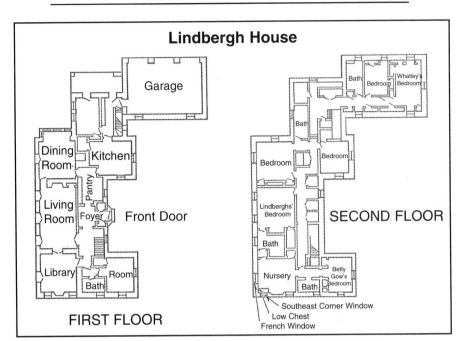

Lindbergh House

Garage

Bath | Bedroom | Whatley's Bedroom

Bath

Dining Room | Kitchen

Pantry

Bedroom | Bedroom

Living Room | Foyer | Front Door

Lindberghs' Bedroom | SECOND FLOOR

Bath

Library | Room

Bath

Nursery | Betty Gow's Bedroom

Bath

Southeast Corner Window
Low Chest
French Window

FIRST FLOOR

This floor plan of the Lindbergh house shows the location of the baby's nursery, as well as the rooms where his parents and nurse were at the time of the kidnapping.

policeman, arrived, he also saw the envelope and spoke with Lindbergh, asking him if he had any idea who might have committed such a crime. Lindbergh said no. So did the other members of the household who talked briefly with the police. More state policemen arrived, and one of them was directed to read the ransom note aloud. The note demanded $50,000 in ransom money, and warned the Lindberghs not to involve the police.

Now it was official. Baby Lindy, the Eaglet, had been kidnapped.

The first ransom note, left in the nursery, demanded $50,000 and showed a symbol of circles and holes (at lower right) that would be used to determine the legitimacy of future notes.

Still more police began to arrive. The nursery and the ground outside were searched almost continuously. Within hours, at least two hundred people were wandering around the grounds of the estate. As a result, any footprints or other evidence that may have been left was being destroyed.

What the police did find that night was a set of footprints that went from the abandoned ladder to an old road called Featherbed Lane. The footprints stopped beside marks of automobile tires. In the nursery itself, the window to the right of a fireplace was closed, but not locked. The window was covered by shutters, but only the right shutter was closed. It was on the sill of this window that Lindbergh had found the ransom note. There was a muddy mark on top of a suitcase under the window and another on the floor.

When the sun came up, the police were able to look around the area more thoroughly. Both the footprints and most of the prints on the ladder had been completely wiped out by the growing crowd of officials, media people, and sightseers. A splintered riser and a broken rung were discovered on the lower part of the ladder. Lindbergh thought later that he had heard a cracking sound at around nine-thirty on the night of the kidnapping.[3]

On the morning of March 2, the circus began in earnest. Though there was no television in 1932, most people had radios in their homes, or they gathered at bars and restaurants to hear the news of this sad and shocking story. Newspapers were selling out, and

This aerial shot of the Lindbergh estate shows the location of the baby's window. To the right, a police officer shows how the ladder was placed at the window.

beautiful Sorrel Hill became a crime scene camp. Reporters competed for a chance to be in the select group of press people Lindbergh invited into his living room to tell the story the way he hoped it would be printed. Roads were clogged with press and radio people—at least four hundred before noon on March 2. Radio personality Long John Nebel said,

> Down on the road the cars were bumper to bumper waiting to get in or parked there bumper to bumper. They [the New Jersey State Police] were overwhelmed. So was everyone else. There were hundreds of us walking around that place in a stupor, maybe even a thousand, if you count the folks in the woods.[4]

The police finally took control and began shooing the newspeople and the townspeople off the estate. The small town of Hopewell became as busy and chaotic as Washington, D.C., during a presidential inauguration. Only a small area at the edge of the Lindbergh estate was set aside for reports from a communications center Lindbergh and the police set up in the garage. Rumors flew, and speculation about whether there had been a ransom note went on all night.

By midday on March 2, the newspeople knew about the kidnapping and the ransom note—and soon, so did the whole world.

From 1929 to 1932, there had been twenty-five hundred kidnappings in the United States. This number seems enormous now—and it was enormous then. Kidnappings had reached epidemic proportions. They were often carried out by organized crime members, who kidnapped members of rival gangs. Most kidnapping

2

AMERICA IN THE GREAT DEPRESSION

victims were adults. By 1932, it was not just gangsters who were being kidnapped; wealthy people and prominent professionals were now on the list as well. "Kidnapping was an important symbol for the general lawlessness that seemed to pervade the period of the early 1930s as a population devastated by [the] Depression seemed also beset by a collapse of the instruments of law or the will to lawfulness," wrote author Paula S. Fass.[1]

The Great Depression

Kidnapping was just one example of a general disregard for the law that plagued the United States in the 1920s and 1930s. World War I, which ended in 1918, was the first war fought with modern weapons, and it affected the whole world. So many people were killed and the horrors of modern war were so shocking that the war destroyed the feeling of optimism—the belief that things will turn out for the best—that many people in the United States and Europe had felt in the early years of the twentieth century.

The people of the United States were relieved that World War I was over but were worried that another war might begin. Prohibition—the banning of the sale and distribution of alcohol—was started to end the evils brought about by too much alcohol. But it had not improved the morals of the country as its supporters had hoped it would. It had merely encouraged bootlegging—the illegal smuggling and sale of liquor—by gangs and gangsters, and speakeasies—bars that sold bootleg liquor and encouraged gambling and other illegal acts.

The crash of the stock market in 1929 brought on the start of the Great Depression. Many people were out of work, struggling, and hungry. The worst year of the Depression was 1932. As jobs became scarce, some people became desperate. Kidnapping seemed to be a way to get money quickly and easily. Kidnappers often succeeded, which encouraged other kidnappings. Kidnapping was not a federal offense in 1932. It was investigated by the local and state police departments, not by the Federal Bureau of Investigation (FBI). If the kidnappers did succeed in collecting a ransom, or even if they did not, most simply disappeared afterward.

There was no one who was as well-positioned to attract the attention of kidnappers as Charles Lindbergh.

Lucky Lindy

Lindbergh was a tall young man who had grown up on a farm in Minnesota. He was born on February 4, 1902. His father's parents were immigrants from Sweden, and his mother's parents were from Great Britain. Lindbergh's father, also named Charles, was both a farmer and a politician. Though he and his wife, Evangeline Land, never divorced, they lived apart for most of Charles Lindbergh's childhood. Lindbergh lived with his mother. Though his mother had great ambitions for him, she was very formal. When mother and son said goodnight, they shook hands.[2]

Lindbergh grew up to be shy around women. He never smoked cigarettes or drank alcohol. What he did do was drive fast in cars and on motorbikes—and learn to fly. Flying was not an industry then. It was just beginning to become an ordinary part of people's lives. Barnstorming was popular. Because few people at the time had ever flown in an airplane, they were interested in watching those who had learned to fly. Barnstormers staged theatrical flying exhibitions through rural (farming) districts.

When Lindbergh first started barnstorming, he was afraid of heights. He conquered his fear by doing the very worst of what he was afraid to do. When the plane flew low over a town, he was the copilot who would climb out onto the wing and wave to the people below. He did daring tricks such as "appearing to hang from a wing by his teeth; also of standing upright on the wing, attached to the plane by straps," while the pilot made looping circles through the sky. He also parachuted. Pretty soon, he had earned the title of Daredevil Lindbergh on advertising posters.[3]

In January 1924, Lindbergh joined the army as an air cadet. He was one of only nineteen students to graduate, in 1925, out of a class of 104. Lindbergh ranked first in his class. No new pilots were needed on active duty at that time, but he was commissioned as a second lieutenant in the Air Service Reserve Corps.

When Lindbergh left the army, he had a reputation as a smart and daring pilot. He also had a reputation as one of the most determined and meanest practical jokers ever. He would do things like "turning a hose on in the bed of a sound sleeper, putting shaving cream into the open mouth of a snorer, dousing a sergeant's pillow with skunk 'juice'. . . ."[4]

Flying was Lindbergh's life. In April 1926, he became one of the first pilots to deliver airmail, which could be a risky business in these early years of aviation. In the fall of the same year, Lindbergh heard that a prize of twenty-five thousand dollars would be awarded to the first person to fly nonstop between New York and Paris, France, or vice versa. He could not resist the challenge. Lindbergh was a determined person. He worked very hard to find the money to build a special plane just for the flight across the Atlantic Ocean. He named it the *Spirit of St. Louis* for the

Charles Lindbergh would eventually become perhaps the most recognized celebrity of his day.

hometown of the men who had paid for its construction and the city that was his base as an airmail pilot.

Lindbergh succeeded in the Atlantic crossing, and in winning the prize. To do so, he spent two days and a night in the air—alone! He had no sleep during the thirty-five-hundred-mile flight. Lindbergh could take physical hardship and discomfort better than most people.

This solo flight made Charles Lindbergh an instant hero. He became a "knight in shining armor" and America's greatest celebrity, wrote author Ludovic Kennedy, to people the world over.[5] When he came back to the United States from France, there was a ticker-tape parade in New York City in his honor. A crowd of 3 to 4 million shouting, cheering people lined the streets.

However, "Lucky Lindy," as he was soon called, had undertaken the flight because of the challenge— not to be adored by everybody. He never liked all the attention and the lack of privacy that went along with being famous, even though he was a very good public speaker. He had a natural confidence that led him to become friendly with rich and powerful people. Soon he became very rich himself and, always, very famous.

Enter Anne Morrow

One of the rich and powerful people this shy but determined young man met was the American ambassador to Mexico. Dwight Morrow had three daughters and a

LINDBERGH DID IT. TWENTY MINUTES AFTER 10 O'CLOCK TONIGHT SUDDENLY AND SOFTLY THERE SLIPPED OUT OF THE DARKNESS A GRAY-WHITE AIRPLANE AS 25,000 PAIRS OF EYES STRAINED TOWARD IT. AT 10:24 THE *SPIRIT OF ST. LOUIS* LANDED AND LINES OF SOLDIERS, RANKS OF POLICEMEN AND STOUT STEEL FENCES WENT DOWN BEFORE A MAD RUSH AS IRRESISTIBLE AS THE TIDES OF THE OCEAN.

"WELL, I MADE IT," SMILED LINDBERGH, AS THE WHITE MONOPLANE CAME TO A HALT IN THE MIDDLE OF THE FIELD AND THE FIRST VANGUARD REACHED THE PLANE. LINDBERGH MADE A MOVE TO JUMP OUT. TWENTY HANDS HEADED FOR HIM AND LIFTED HIM OUT AS IF HE WERE A BABY. SEVERAL THOUSANDS IN A MINUTE WERE AROUND THE PLANE. THOUSANDS MORE BROKE THE BARRIERS OF IRON RAILS ROUND THE FIELD, CHEERING WILDLY.[6]

New York Times *reporter Edwin L. James was present when Charles Lindbergh landed in Paris after his historic solo flight across the Atlantic Ocean. He gave this report of the landing on May 21, 1927.*

son. The Morrow family was very close and well educated. Morrow suggested that Lindbergh fly a goodwill flight to Mexico in December 1927.[7] Then he invited the young aviator to be a guest at his home. It was at the Morrows' home in Mexico that Charles Lindbergh met the ambassador's daughter Anne Morrow, a small, quiet woman who liked to listen to music and read books. She wanted to be a writer.

Anne had her first flying experience with Charles Lindbergh. She fell in love with flying—and with Charles Lindbergh. She would later accompany Lindbergh on many "firsts" on unusual flying routes around the world. She said that "flying gave you a passport to the secret places of the earth."[8]

Back in the United States, because Lindbergh was so famous, the young couple had to hide their wedding plans. Reporters were camped at the gate of Next Day Hill, Anne's parents' home in Englewood, New Jersey, as soon as the engagement was announced. One day, some friends and relatives arrived for what they thought was a reception for Lindbergh's visiting mother. Suddenly, Anne came into the room in a wedding dress! After the wedding, Charles and Anne Lindbergh changed into clothes they had worn earlier in the day. They left on a usual afternoon drive, waving to the reporters. Then they managed to escape from the press and climb aboard a boat to head for their honeymoon in Maine.

Though they had eluded the press at their wedding, the Lindberghs would remain the most famous couple

Charles and Anne Morrow Lindbergh often took daring flights all over the world together. This photo was taken in January 1930.

in the United States. The birth of their first child, Charles Lindbergh, Jr., on June 22, 1930, was welcomed by the family—and by the world. Radio programs spread the news. Within the hour, a song about the event had been composed and broadcast. But the family and the press were not the only ones to take notice of the birth of Charles Lindbergh, Jr. Baby Lindy's presence was also noticed by the person or people who would become his kidnappers.

A_{fter} the Lindbergh baby's disappearance on March 1, 1932, it seemed that the entire country became involved in the search for little Charlie. People in the East, Midwest, and West looked into abandoned houses and shacks in the woods, just in case the Lindbergh baby might have been hidden there. In the neighborhoods surrounding Sorrel Hill,

NEWSPAPERS, RADIOS, AND GO-BETWEENS

police talked with countless people. Those questioned included residents of the area, all the construction workers who had worked on the Lindbergh house, anyone who could identify people traveling into Mercer or Hunterdon counties in New Jersey, and, of course, local telephone operators who might have picked up a call. All the servants who worked at both Sorrel Hill and Next Day Hill (the Morrow estate) were under suspicion, especially Charlie's nurse, Betty Gow.

The Search Begins
Cars traveling across the George Washington Bridge and all other bridges and tunnels from New Jersey to

New York City were searched. All boats entering or leaving harbors in the East were boarded and searched by waterfront police. Reports of little Charlie's being seen with strangers began to pour in to the little town of Hopewell from all over the country. All of these had to be checked. Gangs wanting to get even with other gangs made anonymous phone calls naming suspects and places the baby was being held. When the police arrived they found illegal liquor dumps. One man with New Jersey license plates, who was on his way to California, was pulled over 107 times![1]

The media, whose job is to report news, had few facts to go on. So, they made up their stories. When they could not get news about the kidnapping, they interviewed and took pictures of people reading and listening to news about the kidnapping. The little town of Hopewell increased its revenue, but mourned its gardens, which were trampled on, as was the privacy of its people by news crews who were determined to get a scoop.

Meanwhile, the entire investigation was being run out of the Lindbergh estate. The garage was turned into a police station, complete with a switchboard. "It is impossible to describe the confusion," Anne wrote her mother-in-law on Saturday, March 5,

> —a police station downstairs by day—detectives, police, secret service men swarming in and out—mattresses all over the dining room and other rooms at night. At any time I may be routed out of my bed so that a group of detectives may have a conference in the room.[2]

This map shows the location of the Lindbergh estate in relation to the Hopewell, New Jersey area, as well as the places in which certain pieces of evidence were found.

Charles Lindbergh, a man who was used to taking over in a crisis, tried to control the amount of information and the extent of police involvement. He did not want to scare off the kidnappers. He believed that nothing should be allowed to jeopardize finding the baby and paying the ransom.[3] His behavior and desire to lead the investigation put him in conflict with the New Jersey State Police, headed by Colonel H. Norman Schwarzkopf, a former army colonel whose son, Norman Schwarzkopf, Jr., would become famous as the victorious general in the Persian Gulf War nearly sixty years later.

SS. SIMON AND JUDE SCHOOL.

Police are supposed to solve crimes and arrest criminals. Because Lindbergh was America's hero, however, the police informed other bureaus all over the country that,

> the arrest of the kidnappers is a subordinate consideration, and any member of the Force is authorized to enter into personal and confidential negotiations for the safe return of the infant without responsibility for the detection or arrest of the kidnappers.[4]

Lindbergh formed a sort of committee, which included his trusted friend and lawyer Henry Breckinridge, Colonel Schwarzkopf, and "Wild Bill" Donovan, who was about to run for governor of New York State. The men put a message on the front page of all the local and some of the national newspapers about what the baby should be eating. (At the time of the kidnapping, the baby was recovering from a cold, and was on a special diet for health reasons.) The next day, they pledged that any meetings between the kidnappers and whomever Lindbergh chose to represent him would be confidential.

Contacting the Underworld

Given the times, the underworld quickly became interested in the kidnapping case. Lindbergh was aware of a famous case in which an adult heiress named Nell Donnelly was kidnapped by one gang and retrieved by another gang. The gangsters did not like all the publicity being showered on them, because it meant they might be discovered doing other illegal things. They made sure that the heiress was returned, unharmed and without a ransom, to her family.

A representative of one of the underworld gangs contacted Lindbergh. His name was Morris "Mickey" Rossner. Claiming he had a great many connections among gangsters, he proposed to contact the underworld. His services were expensive. Still, Lindbergh decided to employ Rossner and gave him the ransom note. The ransom note was then shown around the underworld.

The effect was negative. Another ransom note arrived on March 5, 1932. The kidnappers, angered at all the publicity, asked for more money—$70,000. The note assured Lindbergh that the baby was being cared for and was being given food based on the diet published in the newspaper. Word was out in the press that Lindbergh had requested underworld involvement. Religious organizations were outraged. Despite reports from Rossner that he had made progress, it became apparent that the kidnapper or kidnappers were not professional gangsters. All Rossner's activities succeeded in doing was to allow any extortionist to join the group demanding money for the safe return of the Lindbergh baby.

A Go-Between Is Chosen

Because publicity about the kidnapping was so extensive, many people wanted to serve as a go-between, someone who would be in contact with both

Lindbergh and the kidnappers. Dr. John F. Condon was one who succeeded. Condon lived in the Bronx, New York City. He was a retired public school teacher who, at age seventy-two, taught twice a week at Fordham University. Condon loved being on display, proclaiming his love of America and the Bronx and frequently writing letters to the editors of newspapers. Condon's local newspaper was the *Bronx Home News*. He sent a letter to the editor, saying he would be happy to become a go-between in the Lindbergh case. He even offered to add one thousand dollars of his own money to the ransom. Condon's offer appeared on the front page of the newspaper, but it was seen only very locally. It did not seem likely to anyone that the kidnappers would pick up the *Bronx Home News*.

However, on March 9, the day after Condon's letter appeared in the newspaper, an envelope was waiting for Condon. Inside the envelope was a note and another envelope. The note read:

> Dear Sir: If you are willing to act as go-between in Lindbergh case pleace follow stricly instructions. Handel incloced letter personaly to Mr. Lindbergh. It will explain everything. Don't tell anyone about it. As soon we found the Press or Police is notifyed everything are cansell and it will be a further delay. After ytou gett the mony from Mr. Lindbergh put these 3 words in the New York American
>
> Money is redy
>
> After notise we will give you further instruction. Don't be affrait we are not out fore your 1000 $ keep it. Only act strickly. Be at home every night between 6 12—by this time you will hear from us.[5]

SOURCE DOCUMENT

Dr. John Condon received this envelope with a letter that told him to get involved in the kidnapping case as a go-between.

Condon was shocked. He went to a restaurant and showed the letter to two friends. They told him to call Lindbergh at Hopewell. When Condon called, he talked to Robert Thayer, a lawyer connected with Bill Donovan. Thayer thought the wording of the letter was similar to that in the ransom note that had been found at the Lindbergh estate. He asked Condon to come to Hopewell immediately.

Condon arrived with his friends at around two in the morning. Lindbergh and Henry Breckinridge read the note. They, too, thought it was similar enough to the first note to be the real thing. Condon was invited to stay the night. In later years, Condon wrote lots of dialogue about what happened that night and afterward.

Condon's tendency to exaggerate confused matters, however, because he often enhanced and dramatized conversations.

Jafsie

Lindbergh accepted John Condon as the go-between. It was very important that the press not find out about this, because that might scare the kidnappers. Therefore, an alias, or false name, was necessary for Condon if he were to place the ad in the *New York American*. Condon chose "Jafsie"—the sound of his initials, J.F.C., when spoken together. Breckinridge took Condon home to the Bronx, and became Jafsie's houseguest—probably to keep an eye on him. This was indeed an odd, untested connection!

The ad was placed and the same day, a call came in. Condon spoke to a man who had a thick accent, either German or Scandinavian. In the background, Condon said he heard Italian being spoken. The next night, a taxi driver came to Decatur Avenue with a note. Condon and Breckinridge asked the taxi driver to wait while they opened the note. The taxi driver, Joseph Perrone, said he could not describe the man who had hailed him and given him a dollar to deliver the envelope. The note gave Condon instructions for picking up further instructions.

Condon was directed to go to the main gates of Woodlawn Cemetery. Though the ad had said "Money is Ready," Condon went in without the money. It had taken time to get together that much cash. This was during the Great Depression. Even though Lindbergh was wealthy, he had to sell his stocks at about one fifth of their value to get $70,000 for the ransom money. Condon also thought it was necessary to get some evidence that the baby was still alive or that the kidnappers even had him, before paying the money.

It was cold and dark on the night of March 12, 1932. The cemetery and its tall iron gates looked menacing. Condon had been driven there by his friend Al Reich. "When they shoot you tonight," Reich grumbled, "they won't have to carry you too far to bury you."[6] Condon refused Reich's offer to go with him and waited alone for a long time at the cemetery gates.

"Jafsie" Condon met the supposed kidnapper, whom he called "Cemetery John" at Woodlawn Cemetery, seen here.

At first, nothing happened, but then, a man signaled with a white handkerchief. About what happened next we have only Condon's words, reported with much flourish years later. It seems that Condon made contact with a man who called himself "John" and who was a member of "the gang" that had supposedly kidnapped Baby Lindy. John assured Condon that the baby was all right. To prove it, John agreed to send the baby's sleeping suit to Condon. He told Condon that little Charlie was being held on a boat, and that, because of all the publicity, they required $70,000 ransom. John also told Jafsie to put an ad in the *Bronx Home News* stating, "Baby is Alive and Well, Money is Ready." This was to signal the people holding the baby on the boat that everything was set for the exchange of the baby and the ransom.

The ad was placed and appeared on March 13 and 14. Two days later, the sleeping suit arrived in the mail. Lindbergh disguised himself so reporters would not follow him and went to Condon's home to identify the suit. A Dr. Denton's size 2 baby's pajama suit was in the package. Lindbergh identified it, absolutely, as the one his son had been wearing on the night of March 1.

On the two previous ransom notes there had been a red and blue symbol, in a circle. Another such note was attached to the pajamas. It said that the baby was well, but that no more conferences would be allowed. An ad must be placed that said: "I accept, money is redy." When the money was received, the kidnappers would inform Lindbergh, after eight hours, where to find the baby.

Condon felt they should not hand over any money until they had proof that the baby was still alive. No one, however, insisted that the kidnappers take the baby's fingerprints and send them to compare with fingerprints from his favorite toys. From a modern standpoint, this seems to be a very serious oversight.

During this time, the ransom money was being put together. At first, Lindbergh refused the idea of making a record of the serial numbers of the bills. But Elmer Irey of the United States Treasury insisted that, at the very least, they record the serial numbers of notes and make most of the notes gold certificate bills. Gold certificate bills were paper money guaranteed by an equal amount of actual gold. They were easier to locate because there had been fewer of them issued than ordinary bills. Lindbergh agreed, though he still insisted that no police be involved in the ransom money drop.

Several other contacts by note with the kidnappers occurred that stressed the strength and planning of the kidnapping scheme. Odd salespeople—who offered goods and services to Condon, but to no other neighborhood houses—began to turn up at Condon's door, making it appear that members of the kidnapping gang were watching "Jafsie." Still, Lindbergh refused to have the police check any of this out. On March 31, Condon's ad, "I accept, Money is Ready, Jafsie," was placed in the *New York American*.

John Condon's Bronx home, seen here as it looks today, became the center of some of the strangest events of the Lindbergh kidnapping case.

The ad worked. A note arrived saying the money must be delivered on Saturday, April 2, and that instructions would be given about how it should be done. If Lindbergh and Condon agreed, they should place another ad in the newspaper. This was done and the money assembled.

The Ransom Is Paid

Cemetery John, as Condon called the man he had met at Woodlawn Cemetery, had insisted that the bills be placed in two packages. The ransom should contain $25,000 in twenties, $15,000 in tens, and $10,000 in fives. The packages were divided into small packets of money tied with paper bands from the Morgan bank. The larger packages were wound with string, samples of which were saved in the bank vault in case similar material was found on a suspect. In the larger package were $50,000 in bills, including $36,000 in gold notes. The smaller package held $50 gold certificates. None of the serial numbers were in sequence. There were 5,150 bills in the two packages. Treasury agents and bank clerks took eight hours to assemble, pack, and record the numbers of the ransom money. As soon as it was ready, it was loaded into Al Reich's car, which Lindbergh himself drove to Condon's house.

Lindbergh arrived at Condon's house with his lawyer, Colonel Breckinridge, and the ransom money. At 7:45 P.M., a taxi driver arrived with an envelope, which was handed to Condon's daughter. Condon opened the envelope and read it. Then Condon set out, with Lindbergh driving. The note gave Condon the address of a florist's shop, where he would pick up another note under a table. He was warned not to alert the police, and to follow the instructions in the note. This note told him to "cross the street and walk to the next corner and follow Whittemore Ave to the soud [south] take the money with you. come alone and walk I will meet you."[7]

Whittemore Avenue was on the south end of St. Raymond's Cemetery. Condon showed a lot of courage to plunge forward in the dark onto what was then a small dirt road. At first he did not see anyone. He went back to the car, where Lindbergh waited, and said loudly, "There doesn't seem to be anybody here." Then a voice came from inside the cemetery, saying, "Hey, Doctor, over here."

Condon went into the gloomy cemetery and saw a figure darting in and out between the tombstones. Finally, a voice from behind a bush said, "Hello." It was John, the same man who had been in Woodlawn Cemetery. Condon told John he did not have the money. He said he needed a note to say the baby was all right. He also said he could only give John $50,000—which did not seem to upset the extortionist. In fifteen minutes, John came back with a note, and Condon came back with the ransom. Condon was told that the baby was on a "boad [boat] called Nelly." He was given a note, which he and Lindbergh were not supposed to open for six hours. It would direct them to the boat and the baby.[8]

Condon arrived back at the car. Lindbergh told him that a man in a brown suit had run down the other side of the street, but he had not seen his face. Though John had told Condon not to open the envelope for six hours, Lindbergh and Condon opened it a mile from St. Raymond's. The note claimed that the boat *Nelly* was about twenty-eight feet long. On it, with the baby, were two people who were innocent. The boat was supposed to be between Horseneck Beach and Gay Head near Elizabeth Island, off the coast of Massachusetts.

The happiness of the successful mission was diminished when Condon told a representative of the United States Treasury how he had saved Lindbergh $20,000 by getting John to take only the first package with $50,000 in it. The second package had contained $50 gold certificates—the easiest of all to trace!

HOPE WON—AND LOST AGAIN

During the weeks when the notices were appearing in the newspapers in preparation for delivery of the ransom money by Dr. Condon, other would-be go-betweens were trying to get Charles Lindbergh's attention. One of these was Gaston Means, who had used the good reputation of his family, many of whom were governors, mayors, and police chiefs, to get a very bad reputation. He was a con man who cheated people out of money.[1] He had even been tried for murder.

Extortion Plots

Despite these warnings of a bad character, a very rich woman named Evelyn Walsh McLean believed Means when he said he had learned from his mistakes. He claimed that he had even had the advantage, through his criminal past, of knowing the Lindbergh kidnappers. Mrs. McLean, who had lived through kidnapping threats about her own son, gave Means $100,000 to meet the demands of the Lindbergh baby's kidnapper.

By mid-April, she knew that Means was a fraud, and he was tried for extortion. He claimed at that time that he no longer had the money McLean had given him. He said he had paid it to a man named Jorgenson, alias Jacob Nosovitsky.[2] Nosovitsky was a master forger. He had lived by many aliases and had even been employed by the FBI at various times. Though the idea that he was part of the kidnapping and extortion scheme has been written about, no one has ever been able to locate him or prove that he was involved.

In addition to Means, another extortion plot surfaced on March 22. John Hughes Curtis was supposedly a successful businessman. He had convinced H. Dobson-Peacock, a respected minister, and Admiral Guy Burrage, who had been the commander of the United States warship on which Lindbergh returned home after his solo flight to France, that he was an official go-between. Curtis said a man named Sam had been designated by the kidnappers to reach Lindbergh, through Curtis. Burrage and Dobson-Peacock were to help.

Soon the press got wind of this possible link to the kidnappers and claimed that $50,000 was about to be deposited in the names of Curtis, Burrage, and Dobson-Peacock. When the ransom was actually paid by Condon to Cemetery John on April 2, 1932, the press first supposed it was paid to Sam by John Hughes Curtis. The well-concealed negotiations

JEFATURA DE POLICIA

CIUDAD DE MEXICO.

S E suplica cualesquiera información relativa al paradero del niño

CHAS. A. LINDBERGH, Jr.

quien fué secuestrado de su hogar el primero de marzo del presente año.

SEÑAS:

Edad 20 meses; peso 27 a 30 libras; altura 73 centímetros; pelo rubio, ensortijado; ojos azul oscuro; tez blanca; frente grande, ancha; nariz ligeramente remangada; tiene un hoyuelo en la barbilla.

Todo informe se tratará confidencialmente.

Director del Laboratorio
Criminalística e Identificación,

El Jefe de la Policía.

Prof. Benjamín A. Martínez.

Manuel Rubio Oviedo.

The Lindbergh baby kidnapping made news all over the world. This poster requesting help in locating the missing child appeared in Mexico.

carried out by Lindbergh and Condon had succeeded in fooling the press.

Searching for the *Nelly*

Directly after Condon handed over the ransom to John, Lindbergh made arrangements to search by air for the boat *Nelly*. With the cooperation of the United States Navy and Coast Guard, Lindbergh would fly a navy plane that was amphibious, or capable of landing on water. He would land near the *Nelly*, pick up his son, and fly to a landing field in Hicksville, Long Island.

On April 3, at dawn, Lindbergh climbed aboard the navy plane in Bridgeport, Connecticut. Condon went with him. Also on the flight were Lindbergh's lawyer, Henry Breckinridge, and Elmer Irey, the treasury agent who had been responsible for registering the numbers of the ransom bills.

Lindbergh searched all day for the *Nelly*, sweeping low across the water. No boat matching the description John had given was seen from the plane or from the Coast Guard boats that searched the area near the Elizabeth Islands. Lindbergh was disappointed—and angry. John Condon, writing about his role in the ransom negotiations, said that when Lindbergh, flying silently over the area, finally spoke, he told Condon that they had been double-crossed by the kidnappers.[3]

By the morning of April 4, the press was becoming aware of the Jafsie, or Condon, connection. The FBI, which had been left out of the ransom negotiations because kidnapping was not a federal crime in 1932, interviewed Condon and went to St. Raymond's Cemetery. They wanted to see whether John had left any footprints when he leaped over the wall. They found a footprint on top of a grave and made a plaster of Paris cast of it.

With the use of the navy's airplane, Lindbergh searched through the air for his son for two full days. Then he had to tell his wife that the kidnappers had not been truthful. Paying the $50,000 ransom had not resulted in the return of their son. As the days went by, it became harder to keep hope alive. Meanwhile, both Gaston Means and John Hughes Curtis were assuring everyone that they had been in touch with the real kidnappers. Though Means was soon exposed as a fraud, Curtis continued to weave complex stories about his supposed meetings with the kidnappers.

John Hughes Curtis

John Hughes Curtis was highly respected and considered financially successful by all who knew him. When he came to Lindbergh's estate on April 18 with another businessman, E. B. Bruce, he had a long tale to tell. According to Hughes, he had met four members of the gang who still held little Charlie. They were all Scandinavian, and one of them was John—the man in the cemetery who had received the ransom money from Condon. Curtis described the gang members in detail and convinced Charles Lindbergh to check into a hotel in Cape May, New Jersey, where the kidnappers lived. The plan was that they would eventually go out in a boat to where the baby was being held in another boat, and for just $25,000 ransom, Baby Lindy would be returned. The baby was supposedly being kept safe by a nurse, the girlfriend of one of the kidnappers. To clinch the story, Curtis claimed to have seen the ransom money.

The weather was poor, and many trips in several different boats were undertaken with no results. There was always some reason why contact was not made— the weather was bad; the kidnappers had been scared off; the kidnappers had fought among themselves. The result was always no result. Curtis left the various boats every so often to meet with the kidnappers. One of these trips was really to New York City, where he signed a deal for an exclusive story—if the baby were

---

SOURCE DOCUMENT

if the kidnappers of our child are unwilling to deal direct we fully authorize "Salvy" Spitale and Irving Bitz to act as our go-between. We will also follow any other method suggested by the kidnappers that we can be sure will bring the return of our child

Charles A. Lindbergh
Anne Lindbergh

The Lindberghs were desperate to find their baby and put notices in the newspaper like this one, indicating that they would accept any go-between or method of finding their son that the kidnappers would offer.

returned—with the *New York Herald Tribune.* As it turned out, John Hughes Curtis was almost bankrupt and his wife was sick.

How long Curtis would have been able to keep Lindbergh on a boat, desperately hoping that he would find his baby, will never be known. On May 12, 1932, Curtis received an urgent telegram in code from Colonel Schwarzkopf, head of the New Jersey State Police. E. B. Bruce said he would deliver it to Lindbergh in person, along with Lieutenant George L. Richard. Though they could not read the code, by the time they reached the *Cachalot,* the boat Lindbergh was using, moored in Cape May, they knew what radio bulletins, not yet heard by Colonel Lindbergh, had told them. The radios and the evening news were broadcasting alarming, sad, and terrible news. It was up to the three men, Curtis, Richard, and Bruce, one of whom had created a cruel hoax, to break this news to little Charlie Lindbergh's father.

Hope Lost, Forever

In 1932, the countryside around the Lindbergh estate was made up of farmland and thick woods. The smaller back roads were of dirt and were traveled by local people carrying produce, logs, building equipment, and themselves from town to town.

On May 12, at 3:15 P.M., two men were riding in a truck near the little town of Mount Rose, New Jersey. They were carrying a load of timber to Hopewell.

William Allen stopped the truck to go into the woods to relieve himself. His partner, Orville Watson, stayed behind and waited in the truck because it was raining lightly and rather chilly.

A little way into the woods, Allen bent to walk under a tree branch. Looking down, he thought he saw a skull.[4] As he looked closer, he realized he was right. There was a baby in the woods, lying in a shallow grave. He ran back to the truck, calling to his partner. Then they drove to Hopewell to find a policeman. They found Officer Charles Williamson in the barbershop. When the men reported finding the body of a baby, he leaped out of the chair and went to the police station, where he called the New Jersey State Police.

The two truck drivers were asked to show officers where they had made their sad and grisly discovery. Indeed, this was the body of a baby. When any person dies, the body deteriorates rapidly. But enough remained of the physical characteristics of the Lindbergh baby for identification, including the number of teeth, the blond hair, the pronounced dimple in the chin, an overlapping toe, and the flannel fabric of both the T-shirt and diaper that had been sewn by his nurse. Both nurse Betty Gow and Charles Lindbergh identified the remains as those of Charles Lindbergh, Jr. It was not felt necessary for Anne Lindbergh to have to go through such a terrible ordeal, especially considering she was due to have another baby in just three months.

It was discovered that little Charlie had died of an extreme blow to the head and that he had probably died on the very night of the kidnapping. The New Jersey State Police later reenacted the kidnapping. Colonel Schwarzkopf climbed down the ladder from the baby's window. Schwarzkopf weighed about 165 pounds, and he carried a sandbag that weighed the same as the baby had. The ladder broke and the sandbag fell to the ground along with the policeman. Investigators thought that the blow to the baby's head might not have been intentional, but rather the result of the baby's falling from the ladder onto the hard stones below.

Much criticism was heaped on the police for not having searched the area more thoroughly right after the kidnapping. People and press reports said bloodhounds should have been brought in and the services of volunteers accepted.

On May 12 and for several days afterward, the area of the Lindbergh estate and Hopewell once again became crowded with reporters and onlookers. The actual grave site was fenced off by the New Jersey State Police, but the roads were filled with cars, bumper to bumper, carrying eager reporters and curious onlookers.

The accidental discovery of the Lindbergh baby had ended all hope for his parents. It had also ended the cruel extortion plots and the paying of ransom money that would never bring back the Lindberghs' little boy. Since the baby could no longer be harmed, the police were now free to search openly for the kidnappers. A question had to be answered: Were the extortionists also the kidnappers?

John Hughes Curtis, brought back to police headquarters at the Lindbergh estate for questioning, bluffed his way through a few days. The police alternately ignored and harassed him. Finally, he confessed. At first, he said the only lie he had told was that he had actually seen some of the ransom bills in the kidnappers' hands. In the end, he admitted that the whole complicated story had been a complete fib. He claimed he had had a nervous breakdown due to financial and personal troubles. Nonetheless, he was taken to jail. However, because the only crime he had actually committed was obstruction of justice, Curtis ended up with a light sentence that was commuted to a fine. To many people, it seemed much too little consequence for a totally selfish, mean hoax.

The Lindberghs could now begin to repair their shattered lives, grieve for their little firstborn son, and prepare for the arrival of their new baby. In mid-June, they left Hopewell and moved to Anne's parents' estate in Englewood, New Jersey. There, security was better and Anne's family was nearby to comfort them. Perhaps they would finally have peace. On August 16, 1932, Anne Morrow Lindbergh gave birth to a healthy little boy they named Jon.

SUSPECTS, RANSOM NOTES, AND LADDERS

With the discovery of the Lindbergh baby's death, all the leads that had not yet been followed up were reviewed. The staff at the Sorrel Hill estate in Hopewell was questioned again, particularly nurse Betty Gow and her Scandinavian boyfriend, Henry "Red" Johnsen. The staff at the Morrow family's Englewood estate, where the Lindbergh baby had been staying just one day before the kidnapping, was also interviewed.

Violet Sharpe

Of particular concern to the police was a young English maid named Violet Sharpe. She had apparently lied about her whereabouts on the night of the kidnapping. She had also lied about who she had been with. The police questioned her before the May 12 discovery, and then intensively afterward. On May 23, her doctor warned the police that she was ill and weak, having just left the hospital after a bout of pneumonia. The police ignored the warnings. Inspector Harry W.

Walsh, the main detective doing the interviewing, grilled Sharpe repeatedly at the Morrow estate and at police headquarters. He even released information about the discrepancies in her story to the newspapers and investigated her sister, Emily, who had moved back to England.

When Inspector Walsh went to Englewood to interview Violet Sharpe yet again on June 9, it was obvious that she was taking things very hard. She looked thin and ill, her story was just as mixed up as ever, and she eventually became hysterical. Sharpe's doctor was called and Walsh had to give up. But he warned Sharpe that he would see her again the next day—at police headquarters.[1]

The next morning, Walsh called to say that Sharpe would be picked up for more questioning. Sharpe said to the house butler, Septimus Banks, "Walsh wants to question me again. I won't go! I won't! I won't!"[2]

Then she ran out of the room. By the time anyone saw her again, she had taken poison. The frightened servants and Anne Lindbergh's brother, Dwight Morrow, called a doctor and tried to revive her. But it was too late. By the time the doctor and the police arrived, Violet Sharpe was dead.

When this news reached the press, the New Jersey State Police came under more criticism. Headlines such as "Punish Cops Who Drove Morrow Maid to Death!" from American papers and "Disgrace to American Justice" from British ones greeted readers.[3] Things were not going well for the police.

The Search for a Suspect Continues

On May 23, Governor A. Harry Moore of New Jersey had posted a $25,000 reward to be given to anyone who gave information that led to the arrest of the kidnapper or kidnappers. A flyer that showed copies of two of the fifteen ransom notes was sent to prisons and police stations all over the United States. The idea was that inmates' signatures would be compared with the handwriting on the ransom notes. Anyone who was arrested through any police station would also have his or her handwriting examined. The entire packet of ransom notes was sent off to handwriting experts in Washington, D.C., and then to a New York City expert, Albert Osborn. These experts believed that all of the notes had been written by the same person and that certain spellings and word formations proved the note writer was German.

The ladder found at the crime scene was sent to wood technologist Arthur Koehler, who found several things that would later be very important. One was that rung number sixteen had been taken from a different source of wood than the other rungs, and it had been used for something else before becoming part of the ladder. The other thing Koehler found was the source of the lumber used in the rest of the ladder. Since the company that milled the wood, the National Lumber and Millwork Company in the Bronx, did not keep sales receipts, the investigation of the ladder stopped there. However, the employees were put

Here, the ladder leans against the outside wall of the Lindbergh residence. The construction of the ladder would become important during the kidnapping trial.

under constant watch and handwriting samples were taken from each one—just in case.

There seemed to be lots of "just-in-cases" in the investigation. Not the least of these was the continued interviewing, sometimes just plain harassment, of Dr. John Condon. Inspector Walsh believed that there had never been a Cemetery John and that getting the ransom money was the only motive of Condon's offer to be a go-between.[4]

Condon, unlike Curtis, never broke down under severe questioning. He stuck to his story and, though he continued to embroider the truth, was never a serious suspect. In fact, Condon spent, according to his own estimate, $12,000 of his own money going to hundreds of lineups and looking at 37,000 mug shots to try to identify Cemetery John.[5]

The Lindbergh Law

When the baby was kidnapped, kidnapping itself was not a federal crime. For this reason, the FBI's hands were tied in the original investigation. One of the only positive effects of the tragedy was that Congress finally passed a kidnapping bill, called the Lindbergh Law. According to the new law, the FBI could intervene if the person kidnapped had not been returned after a week, because then the kidnappers could be assumed to have crossed state lines. When state lines were crossed, kidnapping became a federal offense. The penalty was life imprisonment. An amendment was passed a year later that stated that if the victim were harmed, the jury could recommend capital punishment. This amendment also allowed the FBI to start investigating within twenty-four hours of the crime.

Conflict Among the Police

The ransom money had been paid in the New York City borough of the Bronx. The New York City police gradually became much more involved. Detective James Finn, who had met Lindbergh earlier, when he was posted to Lindbergh's ticker-tape parade, was asked to be the principal investigator. Finn's efforts to get Schwarzkopf and the New Jersey State Police to cooperate by sending copies of the ransom notes went unanswered, and he was not allowed to attend important meetings. He set up his own office in New York and even had a battle map—a detailed city map in which he stuck pins wherever ransom money showed up. When Finn came on to the case, the New Jersey State Police had been contacted by a psychiatrist named Dr. Dudley Shoenfeld, who had constructed a profile of the kidnapper.

Shoenfeld believed the kidnapper was a German, about forty years old, who had once been in prison. He also believed the kidnapper suffered from schizophrenia. According to Shoenfeld, this supposed kidnapper would be built somewhat like Lindbergh, would be married, would not trust people, and would consider Lindbergh a rival. Shoenfeld even believed that when the kidnapper wrote the last note, which said the baby was on a boat between Horseneck Beach and Gay Head, that the word *gay* had originally been *gun*. To Shoenfeld, this indicated that the kidnapper had perhaps been thinking of Gun Hill Road, a large street in the Bronx that would prove important to the investigation in the future.[6]

Schwarzkopf found the profile intriguing. So did Finn, and the idea of using the Bronx as home base for the kidnapper became stronger. The investigation began to be based more in New York. That did not please the New Jersey State Police.

Finally, the Ransom Money Appears

One major reason that the emphasis of the investigation turned to New York City was the appearance of the ransom money—those gold notes that had been in the package John Condon gave to the man in the cemetery. The first ransom bill appeared on April 5, 1932, at the East River Savings Bank on Manhattan's Upper West Side. It was a $20 gold certificate. A bank teller told a local newspaper about it. This was one of many frustrating leaks to the press that law enforcement had to deal with during the investigation. Of course, the secrecy was ended, and the extortionist was alerted that the police knew ransom money was being spent. Only one more $20 gold certificate surfaced that year.

By the fall of 1932, both $5 and $10 ransom bills had appeared, but the identity of the person or persons spending the bills remained a mystery. Two hundred fifty thousand copies of a large booklet—fifty-seven pages in small lettering—listing all the ransom note numbers was sent to every bank. From April 2 until the end of 1932, twenty-seven of the ransom bills listed had been deposited—two twenties, twenty-one fives, and four tens.

The Great Depression was in full swing, and many people were out of work and fearful that they would never find jobs. How would they feed their families? Because of these bad times, people were hoarding gold. On April 5, 1933, President Franklin Delano Roosevelt, dealing with the desperate conditions of the Great Depression, issued an order. By May 1, 1933, all gold notes, gold bullion, or gold coins totaling more than one hundred dollars must be turned in to a Federal Reserve Bank to be replaced with greenback currency.

During the first three months of 1933, no ransom money showed up. Detective Finn and his counterpart in the FBI, Agent Thomas Sisk, were very happy about this. It might force the hand of the kidnapper because he or she would have to get rid of the gold notes soon, as they would not be spendable in large amounts after May 1. The punishment for hoarding them after that date was a $10,000 fine and a jail sentence.

Finn and Sisk asked bank employees at the Federal Reserve Bank to check the serial numbers of all gold certificates that were turned in against the ransom book. The week before the May 1 deadline, fifty $10 ransom notes were exchanged at the Chemical Bank in Manhattan, and fifty more $5 and $10 notes were turned in at the Manufacturers Trust in Manhattan. But no one remembered who had turned them in!

J. J. Faulkner

On May 1, 1933, $2,980 in gold notes, all at once, were exchanged for greenbacks at the Federal Reserve Bank in New York City. Every single gold note was a ransom bill! The man who signed for the transfer was named J. J. Faulkner, and he gave an address on 149th Street in Manhattan that turned out to be false. Again, no one remembered what this man looked like.

However, by the fall of 1933, a pattern had been established. Most of the bills were being passed on

J. J. Faulkner's signature appeared on the bank deposit slips that accounted for a large portion of the Lindbergh ransom money. The Faulkner lead, however, was never really traced by the police.

Lexington and Third avenues in Manhattan and in Yorkville, a German neighborhood, also in Manhattan. The bills came in slowly, and the police spent much time waiting for them to appear. Detective Finn always personally interviewed the cashier at a bank or a store clerk who had reported a gold note. Not many people remembered who passed the notes, but those who did seemed to describe the same man. He was white, about average height, had a long thin face, blue eyes, high cheekbones, and a pointed chin. He wore a dark suit or top coat and a soft felt hat pulled low over his forehead.

Many of the gold notes passed during this time had been folded lengthwise, and then doubled over, causing them to have eight sections. When the bills were examined by the New York Toxological laboratory, the technicians found small amounts of glycerin and emery on them. The conclusion was that the person who passed the bills used a lathe or a drill press, oiled by glycerin, and had used an emery wheel to grind tools. Also, the bills had a musty odor as if they had been stored someplace damp.

A popular cartoonist of the day, James T. Barryman, drew a picture of the supposed bill passer from a description of Cemetery John by Condon and by Joseph Perrone, the cab driver who had delivered one of the ransom notes to Condon. (Joseph Perrone had originally said he could not describe the man.)[7] The people who had discovered ransom bills said they recognized the man in the drawing as the man who had been in their bank or store.

Because of the focus on Manhattan and the Bronx in the kidnapping investigation, Colonel Schwarzkopf finally had to cooperate with Detective Finn. He allowed him to see evidence that had been collected by the New Jersey State Police, including the ransom bills. Some of the competitiveness between law enforcement agencies stopped—for the moment.

More Ransom Money Appears

An important bill passing occurred at the Loew's Sheridan Theater on November 26, 1933. When challenged by the cashier about the $5 gold certificate, the man who passed it had said, "What's the matter. It's good, ain't it?"[8] He had a heavy German accent, was of average height, and had a pointed chin, according to Miss Cecile Barr, the cashier at the theater. "It's good," she said.[9] Checking the ticket stubs later, Finn found one that was missing. Evidently, the man had only bought the fifty-five-cent ticket to change the bill. He had not attended the show. Barr identified the man from the picture drawn by Barryman.

By January 1934, about $40 in ransom bills were appearing each week. Finn noticed that there were no more fives—only tens were being spent. He hoped that the twenties would appear soon, because they were easier to spot. In March, the New York City police offered a $5 reward for anyone who turned in a gold note. Finn asked all gas station attendants to write down the license plate numbers of people who paid with gold notes.

As more money began appearing, the press once again broke its code of secrecy. No bills appeared in June, July, or August. Finn again contacted the editors of all the local newspapers, and each one promised to keep silent. Just as the policy of secrecy was being enforced, John Condon reported that he thought he saw Cemetery John from a bus in the Bronx. Condon had leaped out of the bus to run after him, but John had disappeared. Condon, never one to pass up an opportunity for glory, told everyone about it, and the press broke *that* story instead of talking further about the passing of ransom bills.

By September, ransom bills began to appear again in upper Manhattan and the Bronx. All were tens and twenties. Hundreds of law enforcement agents were sent around these areas. Finn was sure the net was closing on the elusive kidnapper.

But on September 16, 1934, radio show host Walter Winchell revealed the story. Winchell told millions of listeners that ransom money was once again being passed in Manhattan and the Bronx. Then he scolded New York City bank tellers, saying, "Boys, if you weren't such a bunch of saps and yaps, you'd have already captured the Lindbergh kidnappers."[10]

Investigators from New York and New Jersey and agents from the United States Treasury and the FBI had been working on the case for over two years now. They could only hope that the kidnapper was not listening to Walter Winchell that Sunday night.

6

A Suspect Is Arrested

The gold note that finally enabled the New York City police, the FBI, and the New Jersey State Police to bring in a suspect was passed just one night before Walter Winchell's broadcast. On Saturday night, September 15, 1934, a man in a dark blue 1930 Dodge sedan drove into the gasoline station at Lexington Avenue and 127th Street in Manhattan. It was about 10:00 P.M. The man asked for five gallons of gas, which cost ninety-eight cents. He paid for the gas with a $10 gold note. When the gas station attendant examined the note, the customer, in a German accent, said, "They're all right. Any bank will take them."

Walter Lyle, the attendant, remarked that one did not see many gold certificates anymore.

"No," the man replied. "I only have about a hundred left." When the man drove away, Lyle wrote down the car's license plate number on the bill because, he said later, he thought the bill might be counterfeit.[1]

The gold note showed up on bills from the gas station's night deposit. The Corn Exchange Bank in the

Bronx actually saw two $10 certificates come in on the morning of September 18. One of them had a license plate number written on it. Three gas stations had deposited money at the bank. At one of them, Finn interviewed Walter Lyle, who confirmed that he had written down the license number. Finn called the Motor Vehicle Department. A search was done for license plate number 4U13.41.

This ten-dollar gold certificate bill helped lead to the arrest of the kidnapping suspect. On the left edge of the back side of the bill, the license plate number written by Lyle can be seen in faded ink.

The license plate had been issued to Richard Hauptmann, 1279 East 222nd Street, the Bronx. Finally, the investigators had a suspect and a name. By now, the investigation team numbered sixty. All day on September 18, men in plainclothes went in and out of the area near 222nd Street. The block on which Hauptmann lived was mainly home to workmen and their families. All the wood and stucco houses had well cared for lawns. Number 1279 was not as neat as its neighbors, however, and the yard ended in an unpaved road called Needham Lane. Across Needham Lane was a garage with red doors. Woodlawn Cemetery, where the first meeting between Condon and Cemetery John had taken place, was about six blocks away.

Bruno Richard Hauptmann lived in this house, seen here around 1940, with his wife and their young child.

An Arrest Is Made

A plan for taking Hauptmann into custody took shape the night of September 18 as investigators tried to learn something about him. They knew he was renting the upper-floor apartment with his wife and their nine-month-old son, and that two other families lived on the lower floor. He was thirty-five years old and had no arrest record. He had been born in Germany.

The investigators decided to put Hauptmann's house under surveillance and wait until the next morning—Wednesday, September 19—to catch their suspect. If he knew about them and was armed, they would be ready for him.

When morning arrived, five black sedans were ready to give chase. Hauptmann emerged from his house at 8:15 A.M. He looked quite a bit like the picture that had been circulated of the note passer. He was blond, wore a soft felt hat, and looked like he weighed about one hundred eighty pounds. He wore a blue, double-breasted suit and brown shoes. Hauptmann went to his garage, unlocked it, and then backed his dark blue sedan out onto the street. The license plate numbers read 4U13.41—the same number gas station attendant Walter Lyle had written on the ransom bill. After getting out of the car and padlocking the garage, Hauptmann got in the car and drove away. Three of the five black sedans started after him.

Detective Finn drove one car, Agent Sisk another, and New Jersey police were in the third. They tailed Hauptmann as far as East Tremont Avenue, a busy street. When a street-cleaning truck blocked the way, one of the black sedans pulled around and hemmed in Hauptmann's blue Dodge before it could pull around the truck. As Sergeant John Wallace yanked open the door and slid across the passenger seat, sticking a gun into Hauptmann's ribs, a second black car pulled alongside while another blocked Hauptmann's car from behind.

Hauptmann's reaction was simply to stare at all these men surrounding him and then pull to the curb, shutting off the engine. He was yanked from the car and frisked (searched for weapons). None was found, but his wallet contained money. One of the bills was a $20 gold certificate that bore the serial number of one of the ransom notes.

Questions flew through the air. Hauptmann, confused and frightened, made things worse even while he was still on the street, by changing his story about the gold certificates several times. The atmosphere was frantic. Even though all that was known about the man they had pulled from the car was that he had passed a $10 ransom note, Detective Finn and "others at the scene would later contend that they were already certain Hauptmann was both the abductor and the killer of the child," wrote author Noel Behn.[2] The goal of the men who had apprehended and were about to interrogate Hauptmann was to prove that he was the kidnapper-extortionist, not to find out whether he was innocent or guilty.

The investigation had gone on for too long, it had been too frustrating, and the case was too public. The law enforcement task force was only human. But so was Hauptmann. How could he receive fair treatment and a fair trial under these circumstances? Some people think he did, others think he did not, and the facts themselves are suspect. What is certain is that for the next several days, before any trial could begin, Bruno Richard Hauptmann—guilty or not—was treated as if he were guilty.

The Suspect Is Questioned

While Hauptmann was being arrested, other investigators were searching his apartment. Hauptmann was

This New York City police mugshot of Bruno Hauptmann was taken upon his arrest.

brought in, and he showed the officers a tin box in which he said he had gold money. When this turned out to be coins, rather than notes, the policemen doubled their efforts to find more ransom money, cutting open a mattress and strip-searching Hauptmann. Anna Hauptmann, his wife, came upstairs with their baby, terrified, and asked Hauptmann if he had done something wrong. He told her no, and she was told to leave her nearly wrecked apartment.

Sisk noticed that Hauptmann was looking out the window at the garage. There was an electric wire that went all the way from the bedroom window to this garage across Needham Lane. When confronted with this observation, Hauptmann said he had electrified the garage in order to scare off burglars. He demonstrated by pushing a button so that a light came on in the garage. Investigators went out to the garage and started looking around. They saw a couple of wooden floorboards that looked loose. When they pried the boards up they saw loose dirt. They used a shovel to dig and they hit metal. They lifted up a heavy jar—but it contained only water.

Meanwhile, other detectives had questioned Hauptmann's landlady, who lived downstairs. She showed them two $10 gold certificates that Hauptmann had given her as rent payment. Hauptmann was taken to Detective Finn's police station in lower Manhattan. Although he was arrested but not officially charged with a crime, he was fingerprinted, which is against police procedure today.

Though Hauptmann preferred to be called Richard, the police discovered that his full name was Bruno Richard Hauptmann. No matter how much he objected, the officers began calling him Bruno. That would be the name the press used throughout the entire police and court procedure. Hauptmann was questioned for twelve straight hours and willingly took handwriting tests. When these were sent to handwriting expert Albert Osborn, he was not sure whether they matched the ransom notes. Could they get more samples? The grilling went on, and more samples were taken. Then Osborn called Schwarzkopf at 4:00 A.M. to say he did not believe that Hauptmann had written the ransom notes. The police asked Osborn to look at still more samples.[3]

The police questioned Hauptmann for thirty straight hours. According to Hauptmann, the police began to beat him late in the night. The beatings got worse and worse as his story became more and more believable. Wrote author Noel Behn,

> His alibi hadn't changed, which created a dilemma for the New York City police. They alone had Bruno in custody, and a growing number of senior city cops felt that since there was nothing of which to formally accuse him, they had better let him go before word reached the press that an uncharged suspect was being held. . . . Schwarzkopf and the state police would not hear of it.[4]

Just what did Bruno Richard Hauptmann tell the police during those long hours of interrogation? He told them that he absolutely did not extort money

Many writing samples were taken from Hauptmann after his arrest, which were compared with the handwriting that appeared on the ransom notes.

from Lindbergh and certainly had not kidnapped the baby. When quizzed about dates, he came up with plausible and checkable alibis. On March 1, 1932, the night of the kidnapping itself, he said he had worked at the Majestic Apartments in Manhattan and left there around 5:00 P.M. to take the subway home to the Bronx. He then drove his car to the Frederickson Bakery, where his wife, Anna, worked, to have dinner with her. Hauptmann said he had dinner with Anna there every Tuesday and Friday. They finished dinner, came home, and went to bed. The next day, March 2, 1932, he again took the subway to the Majestic Apartments. The first time he had heard about the

Lindbergh kidnapping was when he read about it in the paper that morning.

Did he know Condon? Was he Cemetery John? How come he could remember what he was doing on April 2, 1932—the night the ransom money was paid? Hauptmann said he was not John, did not know Condon except from what he had read in the newspapers, and he remembered the day because, after working a full shift, he had quit his job at the Majestic that day. Because it was the first Saturday of the month, he had met his friend Hans Kloppenburg, who played guitar. Hauptmann always joined him on the first Saturday of the month to play music. Kloppenburg, as usual, had come to Hauptmann's house and stayed until about midnight.

Hauptmann also said that he had not bought a ticket to Loew's Theater on November 26, 1933. That was his birthday, and he and his wife had had friends over to their house to celebrate. Anna Hauptmann, being questioned in a separate room, confirmed everything her husband had said.

When questioned about the fact that he seemed to have enough money despite not being employed full-time, Hauptmann said he had done well in the stock market. In addition, he had a partner in the fur business. The sealskins the police had found at his apartment were owned jointly by Hauptmann and Isidor Fisch, a man who had gone on a trip to Germany in the winter of 1934, and died there. Hauptmann said openly that he had tried illegally to get into the United States twice before he succeeded. However, he lied when asked if he had a police record in Germany. He also lied about having more gold notes, as the police would soon find out. These lies would turn out to be very costly for Hauptmann.

The Search for Evidence

Just as the interrogators were getting worried that they would either have to charge Hauptmann or let him go—and so far they had nothing to charge him with—a phone call came into headquarters. Detective John Wallace of the New Jersey State Police informed Schwarzkopf that the investigators had found $1,830 worth of ransom money in Hauptmann's garage.

While he was being questioned at the station, the detectives had continued searching Hauptmann's house and garage. One of the detectives had noticed that there was an extra board above the workbench in the garage. It was nailed across two upright boards. When it was pried off, a narrow shelf was revealed. There were two packages on it. Detective James Petrosino opened one of them and found one hundred $10 gold certificates. The second package held eighty-three $10 gold notes.

The search intensified. The garage was practically pulled apart, board by board. Another shelf was found that contained a shellac can holding $11,930 in twelve separate packages. Schwarzkopf had ordered that when the investigators found more money, they should put all the packages back as they were and then bring Anna

Hauptmann to the garage. The detectives, Sergeant Wallace, Detective Petrosino, and Agent Leon Turrou of the FBI, were told to pretend to discover the money as she watched. They wanted to see her reaction. If they were convinced she knew nothing about the money, she would not be charged.

Anna's reaction convinced them.

"Where did this money come from?" she gasped.

"It's Lindbergh money. Where do you think it came from?" Sergeant Wallace asked.

"I know nothing of this."

"Are you sure of that?"

"I am certain! I know nothing!"

"Well, your husband knew about it, that's for sure."[5]

The total amount of money found that day was $13,760, all of it part of the ransom payment. This, along with another package of $840 found later, represented over 25 percent of the ransom money. With this evidence, what more did they want?

The Fisch Story

After the police had found the money, they asked Hauptmann again if he had any more gold notes. By this time, Hauptmann had undergone thirty hours of interrogation while sitting in a hard wooden chair. He continued to lie about the money hidden in the garage, and further condemned himself. When confronted with the fact that police had found the money he said he claimed not to have, he said he had heard them, and was not going to lie anymore. He said he could explain the money. Bruno Richard Hauptmann was charged with possession of stolen property. Other charges would follow.

The story he told came to be called "The Fisch Story." This was for two reasons. One was that Hauptmann's partner in the fur business was named Isidor Fisch. When Fisch went on a trip to Germany, he had asked the Hauptmanns to store some things for him, including a shoe box tied with string. Hauptmann put it on a shelf in a closet in his kitchen and forgot about it. Fisch died of tuberculosis in Germany on March 29, 1934.

Just three weeks before Hauptmann's arrest, there had been a bad rain, and the roof over the closet had leaked. Hauptmann took things out of the closet and found the shoe box, which was wet. He opened it and found, much to his surprise, $14,000 in gold certificates. He never told Anna about the money. Instead, he took it into the garage, rewrapped it, and hid it. When Fisch had left for Germany, he owed Hauptmann about $7,000. So Hauptmann took his loan back, figuring he would spend that and decide later what to do with the rest of the money. He began to spend the $7,000 late in August 1934—just when the money began to reappear around New York.

The second reason Hauptmann's explanation was called "The Fisch Story" was that "at the time no one believed the Fisch story . . . but several of the most cynical officers grudgingly marveled at Bruno's ability to come up with such a yarn after undergoing nonstop interrogation without sleep and food."[6] Sometimes when people catch a large fish, but no one actually sees it, the stories they tell about it get more and more impressive. So the term *fish story* has come to be used any time someone tells a whopping big lie.

But what about this Fisch story? Could it be true? Who was this man, Bruno Richard Hauptmann, whom the world already hated and assumed had extorted money from Charles Lindbergh and killed his young son?

Background of the Suspect

Bruno Richard Hauptmann had been born on November 26, 1899. He was only two years older than Charles Lindbergh. The Hauptmann family lived in Saxony, a part of Germany near what is now the border of the Czech Republic. His father was a stone mason and a farmer. Hauptmann was the youngest of five children.

Hauptmann was close to his mother, but not to his father, who drank heavily and hit him. He went to school until he was fourteen and then was apprenticed to a carpenter. By this time, his elder sister had moved to America and his three older brothers were at the front of the battle lines of World War I. Hauptmann tried to join the army himself, but was too young.

By the time he was called to active duty, in 1918, when he was nineteen years old, two of his older brothers had been killed and the third was missing in action. His parents were heartbroken, afraid of losing another son. But Hauptmann survived, suffering all the usual dangers, discomforts, and humiliations of war. He was wounded twice and spent the last days of World War I in an army hospital.

The missing brother had turned up, so the two Hauptmann brothers returned home in January 1919. Their hometown, however, was not the same as it had been when they left. The Versailles Treaty that ended World War I had forced Germany to pay severe economic reparations (paybacks). Germany became, for some years after World War I, a very poor country. People could not get jobs, and even if they did, food and clothing were hard to come by. As Americans would be doing while the Great Depression was going on in the 1930s, the Germans after World War I wondered how they would feed their families. Desperate measures were often taken.

Hauptmann's solution to this poverty was a dishonest one, and it would come back to haunt him. He stole coal from the one job he could find, in a coal mine. Unable to find another job, he joined a friend who was also hungry and discouraged. They went on a six-day burglary spree. Twice, they climbed into empty houses and stole. The third time, they held up two women at gunpoint for food and money. Then, they burglarized a store and were caught.

For these crimes, Hauptmann was sentenced to prison. He broke out but then went back at his mother's insistence to serve out his stiff sentence. He spent four years in prison before being released and put on probation for three years. When he was in prison, he had vowed never to steal again, but he could not find a job after his release. Again he grew hungry and discouraged, and once again, he stole.

He was returned to prison in 1923. This time, he broke out almost before the gates had closed on him. He did not return. He had long wanted to go to America and had read many books on travel while in prison. He had no money, so he decided to stow away. That is, he would hide on a boat going to America and hope that the boat's officers would not find him and return him to prison.

The first time Hauptmann crossed the ocean as a stowaway, he was discovered early in the voyage. He saw the docks at Hoboken, New Jersey, through a locked cabin window. When he and other stowaways who had been caught were being taken by steamboat to Ellis Island, the major entry point for immigrants, he jumped overboard. He stayed in the water by a pier for nearly nine hours. Then, half frozen, he walked onto the pier, right into the arms of a security guard.

Hauptmann remained on Ellis Island for two weeks before being sent back to Germany. Again, poverty discouraged him and he stowed away for a second time. Some fellow Germans let him sleep on the floor of their cabin. He thought he would make it this time. But one day, when he left the cabin for some air, he ran right into the same officer who had caught him stowing away the first time. Back to Germany Hauptmann went.

Hauptmann almost immediately got back on another boat—for a third try at stowing away. He stayed below decks in the bins where coal was kept. Seven other stowaways turned out to be in the coal bins, too, and they shared food that was brought to them by an accomplice in the kitchen. Covered with coal dust, all they had to do was shut their eyes—so the whites would not show—and lie still if anyone came into the area.

When the boat docked in Hoboken, the stowaways went into the bathrooms and cleaned up, just like the crew. Writing about his life later on, Hauptmann said,

> The passengers had already left the boat while I was still shaving. . . . Now I too walked down the gangplank without being stopped. I reached the pier and from there went into the street. "God, I thank you." These were my first words as I trod the pavements of the New World.[7]

Hauptmann found work, first as a dishwasher, then as a locksmith, and then as a carpenter, in New York. He also became friends with other German immigrants. He met Anna in the summer of 1924, married her a year later, and started a life that included hard work, travel, and companionship. Accustomed to being poor, he was thrifty. Anna worked, too, and they saved their money. Hauptmann did so well at carpentry that he became a member of the Carpenters Union.

The Hauptmanns moved to the Bronx, which, at that time, was just being built up from farmland.

No problem with the law ever came up from the time Hauptmann arrived in the United States in 1924 until he met Isidor Fisch. Fisch, who lived frugally himself, had duped numerous people into financial schemes. Buying "dirty money" for cheaper than its face value, and then spending it at its full value, hoping not to be caught, was something underworld people did frequently during the Great Depression. Though Hauptmann by all rights should not have spent money that was not his, perhaps Isidor Fisch *did*

Isidor Fisch, the friend of Bruno Hauptmann's who may have given the ransom money to Hauptmann, is seen here (second from left) with some friends.

buy the Lindbergh ransom money from one of his underworld connections or was involved in the extortion itself.[8] Perhaps Hauptmann, in his statements to the police, was telling the truth.

Now, ten years after he had arrived in the United States, Hauptmann sat in the interrogation room of the New York Police Department. The number of ransom bills found in his garage was multiplying, and his hopes of release were being diminished. What would the police find out next?

PREPARING FOR TRIAL

In the days following the arrest of Bruno Richard Hauptmann on September 19, 1934, a number of things occurred. First, he was identified by taxi driver Joseph Perrone, who had said earlier that he had not even seen the man who gave him the note for John Condon. On looking at a lineup where Hauptmann was wedged between two beefy policemen, Perrone suddenly claimed to recognize him. John Condon at first said he could not be absolutely sure that Hauptmann was the man. Then he, too, changed his mind. Cecile M. Barr, the cashier at Loew's Theater, identified Hauptmann as the man who had given her the ransom bill. A grocery clerk and Walter Lyle, the attendant at the gas station where the last bill was passed, also identified Hauptmann.

It seemed that enough evidence had been gathered to charge Hauptmann with extortion, though it is unclear what the police were doing to check his alibis at this time. H. Norman Schwarzkopf, the head of the New Jersey State Police, was not satisfied. He needed to get Hauptmann over to the New Jersey side of the Hudson River to be tried there. That would be impossible unless there was enough evidence to build a case for Hauptmann being the kidnapper of the Lindbergh baby as well as the extortionist (the person who had taken the ransom money).

Building a Case

Hauptmann had a record as an honest man and a good worker since arriving in the United States. However, his early robberies and convictions in Germany were against him. One of the burglaries involved putting a ladder up against a second-story window—that did not look good. He had lied about his arrests, had entered America illegally, and had not yet become a citizen. So far, however, there was nothing to link Hauptmann with the kidnapping itself. His lawyer, James Fawcett, had employment records from the Majestic Apartments that proved Hauptmann was working there on the afternoon of the day of the kidnapping—March 1, 1932. How, Schwarzkopf wondered, could Hauptmann possibly be extradited—removed from one state to another for trial—if there was no evidence that he was the kidnapper and he had an alibi for the kidnapping date?

Here is where things got fuzzy. John Condon's home phone number was found written on a beam inside a closet in the nursery of Hauptmann's baby, Manfried. When he was shown the number, Hauptmann indicated that if it was his beam, he must have written the number. Later, he said he did not know that the wood was from a closet. A 1989 television documentary on the Lindbergh case had writer Anthony Scaduto asking, "Why would a man write on the inside of a dark closet the phone number of the intermediary with whom he is dealing in a kidnapping case, if he doesn't have a telephone in his house?"[1]

Planting evidence to get a story was a common occurrence in the 1930s. According to three separate sources, it was journalist Tom Cassidy who actually wrote the phone number on the beam in Hauptmann's house, at first as a joke. Cassidy had even bragged about it.[2]

But it was taken seriously. The next nail in Hauptmann's coffin was Lindbergh's identification of his voice. Hauptmann was directed to say, "Hey, Doctor, over here," in Lindbergh's presence. Though Lindbergh had said earlier that he could not possibly identify the voice he had heard outside the cemetery two years ago, he now claimed to recognize it. This was definitely the man, he said.[3] Lindbergh's popularity and the horror people felt about his baby having been kidnapped and killed, added to the hysterical wish to find a scapegoat. Someone *had* to be guilty!

Hauptmann was indicted by a Bronx grand jury for extortion. No bail was granted. He was portrayed in the media as a monster. It became increasingly difficult for any witness in Hauptmann's favor to get up the nerve to testify. According to writer Noel Behn, after Hauptmann was indicted and returned to jail, investigators went to work on friends and acquaintances of Hauptmann who might have been able to corroborate where he was on critical dates. Nearly everyone but his wife would eventually change what he or she had to say or would refuse to testify in his behalf. Later many of them would claim they had been intimidated, openly threatened, and continually harassed by the interrogators.[4]

The worst threat to a fair trial, bringing with it a certainty that Hauptmann would be extradited to New Jersey and tried for the kidnapping and murder, rather than just extortion, was the disappearance of the employment records of the Majestic Apartments. The records mysteriously disappeared after having been subpoenaed for examination by the New Jersey District Attorney's office. They are among thirty documents that are still missing to this day.[5]

Extradition to New Jersey

The citizens of Hunterdon County, New Jersey, were most eager to have the famous murder case tried there. Revenue followed the reporters, even if gardens suffered. There was a huge cheering crowd in front of the courthouse in Flemington, Hunterdon County, New Jersey, when the grand jury met to hold hearings on the possible indictment of Bruno Richard Hauptmann for kidnapping and murder.

One of the reasons Schwarzkopf had been able to extradite Hauptmann, despite the evidence and the lack of evidence of his being the kidnapper, was because of the appearance of a witness named Millard

*Residents of Hunterdon County were eager to have
Hauptmann face trial in the Hunterdon County
Courthouse, seen here as it looks today.*

Whited. Whited, who lived in a run-down cabin near Sorrel Hill, had been interviewed extensively around the time of the kidnapping. He stated then, and subsequently, that he had not seen anyone in the area the day or evening of the kidnapping or on any other day.[6]

Though Whited was usually unemployed, and had been known to "tell lies as readily as most of us tell the truth," he was to provide the eyewitness account that would justify Hauptmann's extradition.[7] What made Whited suddenly recall what he had said earlier he could not recall? According to writer Noel Behn, "He would later assert that he had been promised three hundred dollars if he would say everything investigators told him and that after he complied, he received only thirty dollars."[8]

At this point in preparing for the trial, the ladder found outside the nursery window on the Lindbergh estate became part of the evidence. Wood expert Arthur Koehler had theorized, while examining the ladder in 1933, that one of the rails had come from an already existing building. Instead of thinking it was a piece of lumber that had been thrown out and then found its way into the building of the ladder, New Jersey Police Detective Lewis Bornmann decided to look in Hauptmann's attic. Eureka! On his second visit to the attic, Bornmann was sure that the flooring looked the same as the rail in question—number sixteen—and he was sure that a plank was missing from Hauptmann's floor. If the police could connect the ladder found at the Lindbergh estate with the flooring in

Hauptmann's house, they could extradite him to New Jersey and charge him with the kidnapping.

Author Ludovic Kennedy, who believed that Hauptmann was not guilty of the kidnapping and murder wrote,

> In all of criminal history there can be few other cases where so much seemingly incriminating circumstantial evidence continued to pile up day after day; yet in which the more the police forces amassed, the more they felt they had to amass, subconsciously aware of the basic flimsiness of their case. . . .[9]

There was such a frenzy—a whirlwind of hate and excitement in the air—that ordinary decency was thrown out the window. A detective even went to Germany to interview Hauptmann's mother. She was away, so he broke into her house and searched it!

All this time, Hauptmann had not budged one inch in his story, no matter how much the investigators wanted him to confess. He had admitted to having the money after its discovery, and told the police why he had it. He stuck to that story, to his alibis, and to his constant and increasingly futile cries of his innocence.

It took the Hunterdon County grand jury exactly thirty minutes to bring in an indictment for murder. The trial was set for January 2, 1935.

8

THE TRIAL OF THE CENTURY

The little town of Flemington, New Jersey, had never seen so much traffic. On the morning of January 2, 1935, the bell in the cupola of the Hunterdon County Courthouse on Main Street pealed within hearing of hundreds of people. Whoever was closest to the courthouse doors had the best chance of getting a seat on this first day of the trial of Bruno Richard Hauptmann for felony-murder. When the courtroom door finally closed on three hundred spectators, one hundred fifty prospective jurors, one hundred reporters, fifty cameramen, twenty-five communications technicians, scores of investigators, and prosecution and defense team members, the trial was ready to begin.

The Trial Begins

The prosecution team was headed by Attorney General David Wilentz of New Jersey, who had been responsible for the extradition. The lead defense lawyer was Edward J. Reilly, a famous attorney who had been nicknamed the Bull of Brooklyn because of his

The Hunterdon County Courthouse in Flemington, New Jersey, became a media circus when the trial began.

aggressive courtroom manner. Reilly was known for self-promotion, and now, as he approached the end of a long and successful career, he was more bluster than substance.[1] The second man on the defense team was Lloyd Fisher, a local attorney with a reputation for directness and honesty. The presiding judge was seventy-one-year-old, dignified, and conservative Honorable Thomas W. Tenchard. What he thought of the carnival atmosphere in his small, packed courtroom on that historic day in 1935 will never be known.

The first weekend of the trial, approximately twenty thousand automobiles and sixty thousand people came to Flemington. Five thousand people pushed past the guards of the courthouse on Sunday, running around the courtroom and all over the building, taking "souvenirs," including toilet paper and pieces of furniture![2]

The Union Hotel, across from the courthouse, had been completely booked since October. At the Union Hotel, one could order a Lindbergh sundae or Baked Beans Wilentz.[3] All over the area, hotel rooms were booked, and one press organization rented an entire country club. In this Great Depression year, local and out-of-town people who had an idea for a souvenir made more money than they thought possible. One local man and his son built miniature ladders resembling the one used in the kidnapping. They were the best sellers of all. What seemed to be forgotten was that this trial would decide whether a man lived or died—and it was happening because a baby had been murdered.

Opening Arguments

Finally, the trial got under way. The many famous people seated in the audience leaned forward in their seats as Bruno Richard Hauptmann was brought in and Colonel Charles Lindbergh came through the door. During the first two days, the jury was chosen and the prosecution made its opening statements. The prosecutor ended by saying, "We will be asking you to impose the death penalty, it is the only suitable punishment in this case."[4]

Defense lawyer Reilly objected strongly to Wilentz's speech, saying that it was a summing up and not an introduction of what the prosecution wanted to prove. He even asked for a mistrial, meaning that a new jury would have to be chosen and the whole procedure started over again. His request was denied.

The Lindberghs' Testimony

None of the spectators left for the lunch break. No one wanted to miss being there when Anne Lindbergh testified. She was led by Wilentz through the events on the night of the kidnapping. When it was the defense's turn, Reilly bowed to her grief and did not cross-examine. The next witness was key to the prosecution: Colonel Charles Lindbergh.

Wilentz asked, "On the night of April 2, 1932, when you were in the vicinity of St. Raymond's Cemetery and prior to delivering the money to Dr. Condon, you heard a voice hollering, 'Hey, Doctor?' I think. Since that time have you heard the same voice?"

"Yes, I have."

"Whose voice was it, Colonel, that you heard in the vicinity of St. Raymond's Cemetery that night, saying, 'Hey, Doctor?'"

"That was Hauptmann's voice," Lindbergh replied matter-of-factly.[5]

The courtroom was in an uproar. When things had calmed down, Reilly cross-examined Lindbergh. This was a hard task, considering Lindbergh was America's hero. Reilly tried to cast blame on servants and on neighbors, but never asked Lindbergh how he could possibly remember a voice he heard so long ago.

In the days that followed, Reilly tried to keep the ladder from being admitted into evidence and was able to make police witnesses look bad. His attempt to discredit Charlie's nurse, Betty Gow, and to implicate other servants and neighbors, did not work. The prosecution brought in more witnesses.

Witnesses for the Prosecution

The first witness David Wilentz brought in was Amandus Hochmuth, an eighty-six-year-old man who lived on the corner of Featherbed Lane, where police had found footprints and tire prints. When questioned, the witness said he had seen a man in a green car go down Featherbed Lane toward the Lindbergh estate on the morning of March 1, 1932. Just as he identified Hauptmann as the driver of that car, the courtroom lights went out.

"It's God's wrath over a lying witness!" shouted Reilly.[6] Of course, the courtroom spectators broke down in shouts and laughter.

In his cross-examination, Reilly resorted to the technique he seemed to be using most often, that of ridiculing the witness. He did the same with Joseph Perrone, the cab driver who had delivered the first note to John Condon. The technique backfired. Reilly looked mean, and the jury liked him less and less.

When John Condon took the stand, Wilentz asked him to identify Hauptmann as the man he called Cemetery John, and he did. Reilly was not able to shake Condon's testimony, and things began to look increasingly bad for Hauptmann. His face had now been identified by three separate men, and his voice by one, the baby's father!

Then the handwriting experts began to appear. The jurors looked sleepy and the crowd was becoming

Charles Lindbergh (in circle at left) attended every day of the trial of Bruno Richard Hauptmann (in circle at right).

restless. Albert Osborn, who had said that Hauptmann had not written any of the ransom notes when Hauptmann was first arrested, now testified that Hauptmann had indeed written the notes. The news headline that day read: "Expert says Hauptmann wrote all the ransom notes."[7]

There had been many rumors that the body found on the hill was not, in fact, that of little Charlie Lindbergh. The big surprise arising from the testimony was that Reilly did not challenge any witnesses who said it was actually Baby Lindy. When Reilly said that the defense had no doubts that the body found belonged to the Lindbergh baby, Lloyd Fisher, the local defense lawyer, jumped from his seat and shouted, "You are conceding Hauptmann to the electric chair!" and left the room.[8]

The prosecution was batting a thousand. They were bringing in many witnesses and much evidence. The newspapers and radio were holding a trial of their own. Walter Winchell, the hard-hitting radio personality who had almost blown the whole case by saying that ransom bills were appearing again in August 1934, had Hauptmann verbally tried, convicted, and electrocuted during the first week of the trial.

Now, more eyewitnesses appeared. One was a neighbor of the Hauptmanns' who claimed that the couple had come back from a trip sometime in March and that Hauptmann was limping with a bruised leg. This statement caused Anna Hauptmann, seated quietly in the courtroom up to that time, to stand up and shout, "Mrs. Achenbach, you are lying!"

After the courtroom settled down again from its usual uproar when something dramatic happened, Anna Hauptmann was scolded by the judge. She promised to keep quiet but said, tearfully, "Well, I will try to do so, but sometimes I can't help it."[9]

Next came Cecile Barr, the cashier at Loew's Theater, who had cashed one of the ransom bills on November 26, 1933. Reilly tried to discredit her testimony but was unsuccessful. This was a bad blow for the defense, because Barr had cashed the note before Isidor Fisch had sailed for Germany. Hauptmann claimed he had not even had the money, never mind spending it, before Fisch left the shoe box with the Hauptmanns on December 2.[10]

The ladder was finally admitted into testimony because of the earlier testimony of eighty-six-year-old Amandus Hochmuth. He had asserted that he had seen a man in a green car with a ladder early on the day of the kidnapping. Hauptmann's car registration showed that his dark blue car had, at one time, been green.

Next on the witness stand were people who had received ransom notes. Then came the wood experts, who testified about rail sixteen of the ladder and the writing in the closet. Millard Whited, the man who had suddenly remembered seeing Hauptmann prowling around the Lindberghs' estate several months before the crime, identified him in court. The prosecution ended with more evidence about the ladder from Arthur Koehler, the wood expert, who impressed the jury with his careful and professional testimony. When a picture of Hauptmann's car was allowed into evidence, Wilentz asked Koehler if he had tried to fit the ladder into that car. Koehler said yes, he had done just that: "When I took the three sections and nested them together, they fit in on top of the front and rear seats, and there were several inches to spare."[11] Then the prosecution rested.

The Defense Makes Its Case

Lloyd Fisher gave the opening statement for the defense. He said the defense team would prove that Hauptmann had an alibi for all the important dates. The defense would bring in handwriting experts who would prove that Hauptmann had not written the ransom notes. They would explain that Hauptmann had done well in the stock market, which explained why he had money, even though he had been mostly unemployed since 1933. In addition, the defense would prove that the evidence about the ladder was worthless. They would tear apart the prosecution's unreliable witnesses and bring in witnesses of their own. It sounded like a good beginning.

In fact, they were able to do none of those things. The employment records from the Majestic Apartments had disappeared. Then, one of the witnesses who said he had other records to prove the existence of the Majestic records suddenly no longer had them, and refused to testify. The handwriting experts dwindled to one who seemed less than believable, and the prosecution witnesses stuck to their stories. The defense's witnesses either refused to appear, were not asked relevant questions by Reilly, or proved to have backgrounds that made them seem unreliable themselves.

On the first day of the defense's turn to present evidence, however, prosecutor David Wilentz must have been a little worried. When Bruno Richard Hauptmann was brought to the stand, Reilly questioned him in a professional way about all the positive aspects of his life, his family, and about his dealings with Isidor Fisch. If, indeed, the "Fisch Story" were true—that Fisch had handed Hauptmann the shoe box full of money as late as December 2, 1933—then this whole trial would be ridiculous. Hauptmann was asked if any of the ransom notes were his, and if he had ever seen little Charlie's sleeping suit. His answer to all of those questions was no, and he repeated that he was innocent. The exchange about the ladder, key to so much of the prosecution's evidence, ended the defense's questioning of the accused.

> "Did you build that ladder?" questioned Reilly.
> Hauptmann smiled.
> "I am a carpenter," he said.
> "Did you build this ladder?"
> "Certainly not."
> "Well, come down and look at it, please."
> Hauptmann did so and, heartened by the response to his first comment, said, "Looks like a music instrument."

Wilentz asked for a repeat of that statement [from his seat at the prosecutor's table].

"He says, in his opinion," said Reilly, "it looks like a music instrument." Turning to Hauptmann [he said], "In your opinion does it look like a well-made ladder?"

"To me," said Hauptmann, "it hardly looks like a ladder at all." He observed the eighteen-inch gap between the rungs. "I don't know how a man can step up."[12]

On the second day of the trial, there was a huge snowstorm in little, crowded Flemington. The court-room was more packed than ever, with people standing

After entering the United States as an illegal immigrant, Hauptmann used these tools in his work as a skilled carpenter. The defense tried to use his woodworking expertise to show that he could not have made such a badly constructed ladder as that used in the kidnapping.

in the aisles and up against the windows to watch this man whom the media had condemned as a monster long before the trial began.

Comedian Jack Benny, one of the frequent spectators, was asked after the first day of Hauptmann's testimony what he thought of the trial. Benny said, "What Bruno needs is a second act," meaning that in this trial, which seemed like a dramatic play, the first act was not going well for the man on trial.[13]

Hauptmann Is Cross-examined

Part of the drama of District Attorney David Wilentz's cross-examination of Bruno Richard Hauptmann was that both were immigrants. One was Jewish and the other German. During this period between World War I and World War II, anti-German feeling was strong in the United States. Anti-Semitism—prejudice against people simply because they are Jewish—had been a constant threat throughout the history of Europe. In both Germany and the United States, Jewish people had risen to positions of power in the 1920s and 1930s. Now, here was a trial in which two members of these historically opposed ethnic groups were facing each other.

Wilentz, though not an experienced prosecutor at the time, was as ruthless as defense attorney Reilly had been in his younger days. In his cross-examination, Wilentz emphasized the fact that Hauptmann had not always been honest:

"Didn't you swear to untruths in the courthouse? Didn't you lie under oath time and time again? Didn't you?"

"I did not."

"You did not?"

"No."

"When you were arrested with this Lindbergh money, and you had a twenty-dollar bill, Lindbergh ransom money, did they ask you where you got it? Did they ask you?"

"They did."

"Did you lie to them or did you tell them the truth?"

"I said not the truth."

"You lied, didn't you?"

"Yes."

"Lies, lies, lies about Lindbergh ransom money, isn't that right?"

"Well, you lied to me, too."

"Yes? Where and when?"

"Right in this courtroom here."[14]

Finally, the defense lawyers objected to the badgering of the witness and Wilentz stepped down. Next, he tried to discredit Anna Hauptmann by saying she must have noticed the shoe box in her very own closet—if it were there! There was, however, one very frustrating thing for the prosecution. Not once, despite the goading, did Hauptmann change a word of his story. Worst of all, he never confessed.

On the morning of February 2, the judge silenced the court because of a whirring sound. It was discovered that newsreel cameras, banned from the courtroom since the start, had been cleverly concealed and were recording the entire trial! Both Wilentz and Reilly swore they had no idea that this was going on, but it was noted that they both had a habit of facing the exact direction of the concealed cameras.

Closing Arguments

Finally, after a six-week trial characterized by a circus-like atmosphere in the streets, in the hotel where the jury was staying, and even in the courtroom itself, it was time for the speeches summing up the evidence. Reilly pointed out, through a long and detailed speech, that all the evidence against Hauptmann was circumstantial (important, but not necessary or essential) and that the media frenzy made an unbiased judgment impossible.

Basically, Reilly claimed that not one shred of evidence indicated that Hauptmann was guilty of anything but passing ransom gold notes—which was not in itself a crime. And yet the "mob" wanted so much to find a scapegoat that they were screaming to kill this German carpenter. They did not care whether he were innocent or guilty. And, Reilly said, he believed Hauptmann was innocent.

Wilentz, on the other hand, became the champion of almost all Americans. He dealt with the anger about the horrible kidnapping and death as if it were obvious that Hauptmann, just from his very appearance and character, had to be guilty.

The Verdict

While people waited for the jury to reach a verdict, a crowd gathered outside the courtroom, shouting, "Kill Hauptmann. Kill the German. Kill Hauptmann." At 10:20 P.M., the courthouse bell tolled, announcing a verdict. The courtroom doors were locked and the curtains drawn. Hauptmann was led in, and, according to writer Ludovic Kennedy,

> people noticed how deathly white he looked and how prominent were his cheekbones. Anna, pale and exhausted, moved nearer to him, and they exchanged a few words. . . . Fisher leaned over and said, "Don't show a sign, because if you do, it will count against you. And remember, whatever the verdict, this is only the beginning."[15]

"Mr. Foreman," said the court clerk, "do you find the defendant, Bruno Richard Hauptmann, guilty or not guilty?"

"Guilty," he said. "We find the defendant Bruno Richard Hauptmann guilty of murder in the first degree."[16]

Then, it was up to the judge to impose the sentence: "Bruno Richard Hauptmann, you have been convicted of murder in the first degree. The sentence of the court is that you, the said Bruno Richard Hauptmann, suffer death at the time and place and in the manner provided by law."[17]

The trial of the century was over.

First Lady Eleanor Roosevelt, commenting on the trial, said, "The entire trial has left me with a question in my mind." Clarence Darrow, a famous lawyer of the time, felt that "no man should be executed on such flimsy evidence."[1]

THE APPEALS PROCESS

Appealing the Conviction

Bruno Richard Hauptmann, on the day after he was sentenced, gave an interview in front of a newsreel camera. He said,

> I want to tell the people of America, that I am absolute innocent of the crime of the murder. My conviction was a great surprise. I never saw the Lindenbergh [*sic*] baby and I never received any money. I want to appeal to all people everywhere to aid me at this time. A defense must be raised to carry my appeal to a higher court. Before God, I am absolute innocent. I have told all I know about the crime.[2]

In another interview in his cell at Trenton State Prison, he told reporters, "If they came to the door and opened it and said, you can go free if you tell the whole truth, I couldn't tell them anything because I have already told the whole truth."[3]

A *New York Times* reporter went to Germany to interview Hauptmann's seventy-year-old mother. She told him, "I know my son is not guilty, but Lindbergh wanted it, and so everything went that way."[4]

It was felt that Charles Lindbergh's presence at all thirty-three days of the trial was one of the reasons it was hard for the jury to bring in anything but a guilty verdict. Other problems that the defense team brought up, as they prepared to appeal the verdict, was that the language the judge used was weighted against Hauptmann and that Reilly had never taken his client seriously. The Hauptmanns, now completely penniless, fired Reilly. Lloyd Fisher would lead the appeal. Though Reilly claimed that he still believed in Hauptmann's innocence, he also indicated that, despite the fact that the Hauptmanns had no money, "Lawyers must be paid. Whether Anna likes it or not, she is going to pay, and pay through the nose."[5] Fisher and Frederick Pope, another defense lawyer, would continue to defend Hauptmann without charging a fee.

While Hauptmann sat in his cell on Death Row at Trenton State Prison, the many people who believed Hauptmann was innocent held rallies to raise funds for his appeal. Anna Hauptmann, her life shattered, spoke at most of these rallies, with her little boy, Manfried, at her side. Many of these rallies took place in German-speaking communities all over the country. The Lindbergh kidnapping case took place during a period of widespread anti-German sentiment in the United States. Many people blamed Germany for having started

World War I and disliked those of German heritage. For this reason, the German communities in America may have supported Hauptmann, who, like the rest of them, was a target of ethnic prejudice.

The Court of Error and Appeals of the State of New Jersey heard the defense appeal. Seven judges from the state Supreme Court and four citizen members gathered in the State House in Trenton. Reporters were allowed in the room, but not photographers. The Hauptmanns were not allowed to be present. The defense brought up the questionable legality of calling the crime first-degree murder, because no witness actually saw Hauptmann kill the Lindbergh baby. The defense team also objected to the closing statement of David Wilentz, which they felt was meant to inflame the jury rather than to sum up the evidence. They particularly pointed to the actions of the judge, whose language was biased and who, they said, never should have admitted the ladder as evidence. They spoke of the unreliable witnesses, the carnival-like environment during the trial, and the presence of Charles Lindbergh in the courtroom. They summed up by saying that, actually, the evidence was *against* the verdict, and the verdict should clearly be not guilty.

Wilentz had a chance for rebuttal against the defense claims. Once again, he was very emotional as he defended his witnesses, the trial atmosphere, and Lindbergh's presence in court.

The judges would have the whole summer to look over the appeal papers, and then they would give their verdict. Anna and Bruno Richard Hauptmann believed the appeal would set him free. In a letter to his wife, written in English because of prison regulations, Hauptmann wrote:

> Dear Anny, when I say I am positive sure, that I have to come home free, is based on my belief in God. . . . Because the State must be responsible on the group of men who was working only in their own interest and not in the course of justice. . . . Therefore this false sentence never will stand, not before God and not before the American nation.[6]

But it did. In a twelve-thousand-word judgment, the Court of Errors and Appeals upheld the guilty verdict, with its sentence of capital punishment.

Governor Hoffman Gets Involved

At this point in the appeal process, a man who, at age thirty-nine, was the youngest governor in the country, became involved. Governor Harold G. Hoffman of New Jersey was an energetic, ambitious man. He had been contacted by several people he respected who felt that Hauptmann had not received a fair trial. Hauptmann repeatedly asked to see the governor, who was the only man who could order a stay of execution (a postponement of the execution date) and recommend to the Court of Pardons, the legal body with the final word on sentencing, that Hauptmann be pardoned.

Hoffman stayed in Hauptmann's cell for a full hour, longer than Hauptmann's own lawyer, Reilly, had ever spent talking with him in four months.[7] Hauptmann had read over the trial testimony in detail. He did not ask for mercy. Instead, he asked that further investigation be done on numerous details that he brought up to the governor. Hoffman went home that night and wrote everything he could remember about his interview with Hauptmann. Hoffman later said: "His story and his unanswered questions put new doubts in my mind and aided in fashioning a firm resolution to search out, within the limits of my resources and my ability, the truth and the whole truth in this mysterious and challenging case."[8]

Due to the governor's efforts, another Court of Pardons was convened, and yet another. On January 16, just one day before the date set for Hauptmann's execution, Governor Hoffman granted a thirty-day reprieve. He also issued a statement that put him in conflict with the police and the media, who had been so sure Hauptmann was guilty all along:

> I do wonder what part passion and prejudice played in the conviction of a man who was previously tried and convicted in the columns of many of our newspapers. I do, on the basis of evidence that is in my hands, question the truthfulness and mental competency of some of the chief witnesses for the state. . . .[9]

End of the Appeals Process

On March 30, *another* appeal was refused by the Court of Pardons. Time was running out. When urged to eat his last meal, "Hauptmann suggested he send it to

This is the electric chair in which Bruno Richard Hauptmann was executed in 1936.

Condon."[10] The day before it seemed he must eat his last meal, Hauptmann had written a letter of thanks to Governor Hoffman for all he had done to try to set him free. He had also warned Attorney General Wilentz, "I swear by God that you convicted an innocent man. Once you will stand before the same judge to whom I go in a few hours. . . . God will be judge between me and you. . . . this case is not solved, it only adds another dead to the Lindbergh case."[11]

A last-ditch stay of execution occurred on March 31 because of a confession by a man who turned out to be innocent. Anna Hauptmann, hearing the news at so late a date, was convinced that this meant her husband had at last been declared innocent. When this, too, turned out to be only a cruel postponement, it made her husband's death even harder to bear. On April 3, 1936, at 8:45 P.M., Bruno Richard Hauptmann died in the electric chair.

★10★

CASE NOT CLOSED

The Lindbergh baby kidnapping is referred to as an unsolved mystery, even though a man was arrested, convicted, and executed for murder. There were many questions left unanswered at the time of Bruno Richard Hauptmann's execution. The fact that the murdered baby was the son of the most famous man in the United States caused people to feel personally outraged about the crime. The desire to get revenge, to feel better because someone had paid for this hideous crime, had clouded people's sense of fairness. "The press on the whole behaved despicably," wrote author Noel Behn.[1]

It is hard to believe that people could be so caught up in their desire to get even with the murderer that they would lie about something that could kill an innocent man. But that has been proven to be the case. Hauptmann may have been guilty, but the evidence at the trial, all of which was circumstantial, did not prove him so.

What Really Happened?

Why did people who, at first, said they could not recognize the face or voice of the extortionist or the gold note passer suddenly recognize him in court? Why did the handwriting expert, Albert Osborn, change his testimony? What happened to the time sheets of the Majestic Apartments, where Hauptmann said he had worked on the very day of the kidnapping? Why was the signature of J. J. Faulkner on more than two thousand dollars' worth of the gold notes exchanged not investigated more thoroughly? Why was evidence about rail sixteen of the ladder only admitted if it could actually corroborate the attic theory? (The difference between rail sixteen and the other ladder rails only mattered if the prosecution could connect rail sixteen with Hauptmann's attic. Why he would tear up a board from his attic when a lumber yard was nearby was never challenged.) Why were there no fingerprints on the ladder or in the nursery? Why was it that the footprints at Sorrel Hill and in St. Raymond's Cemetery did not match Hauptmann's? Why weren't the letters Fisch had written to Hauptmann from Germany admitted into testimony?[2] These and many more questions were left unanswered.

Hauptmann, speaking to Governor Hoffman in his cell, said,

> The poor child haf been kidnapped and murdered, so somebody must die for it. For is the parent not the great flyer? And if somebody does not die for the death of the child, then always the police will be monkeys. So I am the one who is picked out to die.[3]

Bruno Richard Hauptmann had survived three ocean voyages, under conditions that were extremely uncomfortable, to say the least. His criminal past and his ability to lie through intense, if not brutal, interrogation marked him as skilled at not being honest. He had a young baby himself. If he had kidnapped Baby Lindy and then accidentally killed him, would he have been so ashamed that he would prefer to go to his death rather than confess? Perhaps, but the truth remains unknown.

In 1986, Anna Hauptmann, who had lived in poverty following her husband's execution, filed a lawsuit against the state of New Jersey. She was then eighty-seven years old. In the $10 million civil suit, she charged New Jersey officials, including District Attorney David Wilentz, with framing her husband for the Lindbergh kidnapping. Wilentz said that justice had been served and that Anna Hauptmann's claim was "ridiculous" and "absurd."[4] Her claim, like a similar one she filed in 1981, was rejected.

Various writers have advanced theories about what really happened in the Lindbergh kidnapping. Author Noel Behn put forth the theory that there was no kidnapping at all. Behn believed that a member of the family—Anne Lindbergh's sister Elisabeth—was responsible for Baby Lindy's death. According to Behn, in order to protect the family, Charles Lindbergh himself created a hoax. Behn wrote that the extortion plot was totally separate from the kidnapping, and that a man with many aliases, Jacob Nosovitsky, engineered the whole thing.[5] One thing is

Anna Hauptmann spent years trying to prove that her husband was innocent of the Lindbergh kidnapping. She is seen here with criminal investigation expert Robert Hicks.

sure: We will probably never know anything for certain about this still unsolved crime.

The Lindbergh Legacy

After the trial ended, Charles and Anne Lindbergh went on to have five more children and lead a deeply private personal life. Over the years, various people claimed to be the Lindbergh baby, showing up on the Lindberghs' doorstep from time to time.[6]

According to Reeve Lindbergh, the youngest of the Lindbergh children, "I knew almost nothing about the kidnapping while I was growing up. I don't remember ever hearing my parents talk about it—not even once."[7]

The Lindbergh house as it looks today.

The New Jersey State Police Museum near Trenton has created an educational exhibit on the Lindbergh kidnapping, as well as an incredible library of documents and photographs concerning the case. The exhibit emphasizes what is sometimes forgotten in the spectacular events of the investigation, trial, and ongoing confusion about the kidnappers and extortionists. This crime was against a baby, taken from his parents. Reeve Lindbergh said, "More and more, I think of my brother Charles as a real child, rather than as simply a piece of history."[8]

Our times are very different from the 1920s and 1930s. The tremendous excesses of the press, the huge

Today, the New Jersey State Police Museum has exhibits devoted to the Lindbergh baby kidnapping case.

crowds of sightseers treating the kidnapping and trial as if it were a carnival, and the general disrespect for the Lindberghs' private lives, however, remind us of problems that still exist. During the years following the Lindbergh baby kidnapping, America became a virtual circus as it tried to catch and convict the murderer of the Lindbergh baby. More important than whether Bruno Richard Hauptmann was guilty or innocent—something that will probably never be known for sure—is that we learn not to react without thinking. This is how lessons can be learned from history. One of those lessons can be found in the events surrounding the Lindbergh kidnapping.

★ TIMELINE ★

1927—*May 20*: Charles Lindbergh becomes the first person to fly nonstop across the Atlantic alone.

1929—*May 27*: Charles Lindbergh and Anne Morrow marry at Englewood, New Jersey.

1930—*June 22*: Charles Lindbergh, Jr., is born.

1932—*October*: The Lindberghs move into their new house near Hopewell, New Jersey.
March 1: Charles, Jr., is kidnapped; A ransom note demands money.
March 10: John Condon becomes a go-between with the kidnappers.
March 12: Condon meets a man called John at Woodlawn Cemetery in the Bronx, New York.
April 2: Condon gives a ransom of $50,000 to a man in St. Raymond's Cemetery in the Bronx; Lindbergh, in the car, hears a voice shout to Condon.
April 4: Bank teller spots first ransom bill.
May 12: Lindbergh baby found dead in the woods near Hopewell, New Jersey; Police efforts intensify.

1933—*October*: Bruno Richard Hauptmann begins business dealings with Isidor Fisch.
December: Fisch leaves Hauptmann furs, suitcases, and a shoe box and sails for Europe.

1934—*September 16*: Gold certificate bill spent at a gas station is recognized as ransom money; Hauptmann is traced through a license number the attendant wrote on the bill.
September 19: Hauptmann is arrested and ransom money is found hidden in his garage.
September 25: Hauptmann is indicted for extortion by the Bronx grand jury.

October 19: Bronx Court of Appeals denies plea against extradition; Hauptmann is charged with murder and kidnapping and put in jail in Flemington, New Jersey.

1935—*January 2–February 13*: Flemington is overrun by media and spectators as "The Trial of the Century" is held; Charles Lindbergh testifies on January 3; Hauptmann is found guilty of first-degree murder and sentenced to the death penalty.

May 2: Hauptmann makes an appeal to the Court of Errors and Appeals.

October 9: Hauptmann's appeal is rejected.

October 16: Governor Harold Hoffman of New Jersey visits Hauptmann; He leaves doubting that Hauptmann is guilty.

December 21: The Lindberghs leave the United States to live in England.

1936—*January 11*: Hauptmann's death sentence is set for January 17.

January 16: Governor Hoffman grants Hauptmann a thirty-day reprieve.

March 30: Further appeal refused by New Jersey's Court of Pardons.

March 31: Warden postpones execution.

April 3: Hauptmann dies in the electric chair.

★ CHAPTER NOTES ★

Chapter 1. A Famous Baby Disappears

1. Noel Behn, *Lindbergh: The Crime* (New York: The Atlantic Monthly Press, 1994), p. 46; Bessie Mowat Gow, quoted by Charles A. Lindbergh in his statement to the New Jersey State Police, March 11, 1932, Lindbergh Archives, New Jersey State Police.

2. Behn, p. 16.

3. Ludovic Kennedy, *The Airman and the Carpenter* (New York: Viking, 1985), p. 82.

4. Behn, pp. 50–51.

Chapter 2. America in the Great Depression

1. Noel Behn, *Lindbergh: The Crime* (New York: The Atlantic Monthly Press, 1994), p. 381.

2. A. Scott Berg, *Lindbergh* (New York: G. P. Putnam's Sons, 1998), p. 72.

3. Ibid., p. 77.

4. Ludovic Kennedy, *The Airman and the Carpenter* (New York: Viking, 1985), p. 1.

5. Berg, p. 172.

6. Edwin L. James, "Lindbergh Crosses the Atlantic," in David Colbert, ed., *Eyewitness to America: 500 Years of America in the Words of Those Who Saw It Happen* (New York: Pantheon Books, 1997), p. 356.

7. Kennedy, p. 29.

8. Anne Morrow Lindbergh, *Hour of Gold, Hour of Lead: Diaries and Letters 1929–1932* (New York: Harcourt Brace Jovanovich, 1973), p. 252.

Chapter 3. Newspapers, Radios, and Go-Betweens

1. Jim Fisher, *The Lindbergh Case* (New Brunswick, N.J.: Rutgers University Press, 1987), p. 21.

2. Anne Morrow Lindbergh, *Hour of Gold, Hour of Lead: Diaries and Letters 1929–1932* (New York: Harcourt Brace Jovanovich, 1973), p. 229.

3. Ludovic Kennedy, *The Airman and the Carpenter* (New York: Viking, 1985), p. 92.

4. Ibid.

5. Noel Behn, *Lindbergh: The Crime* (New York: The Atlantic Monthly Press, 1994), pp. 96–97.

6. Kennedy, p. 101.

7. Ibid., p. 107.

8. Ibid., pp. 107–108.

Chapter 4. Hope Won—and Lost Again

1. Noel Behn, *Lindbergh: The Crime* (New York: The Atlantic Monthly Press, 1994), pp. 92–93.

2. Ibid., pp. 366–367.

3. John F. Condon, *Jafsie Tells All* (New York: Johnathan Lee, 1936), p. 173.

4. Behn, p. 169.

Chapter 5. Suspects, Ransom Notes, and Ladders

1. Jim Fisher, *The Lindbergh Case* (New Brunswick, N.J.: Rutgers University Press, 1987), p. 150.

2. Ibid., p. 151.

3. Ibid., p. 158.

4. Ibid., p. 163.

5. Ibid., p. 163.

6. John F. Condon, *Jafsie Tells All* (New York: Johnathan Lee, 1936), pp. 190–200.

7. Noel Behn, *Lindbergh: The Crime* (New York: The Atlantic Monthly Press, 1994), p. 202.

8. Fisher, p. 180.

9. Ibid., p. 181.

10. Behn, p. 206.

Chapter 6. A Suspect Is Arrested

1. Noel Behn, *Lindbergh: The Crime* (New York: The Atlantic Monthly Press, 1994), p. 207.

2. Ibid., p. 211.

3. Ludovic Kennedy, *The Airman and the Carpenter* (New York: Viking, 1985), p. 182.

4. Behn, pp. 213–214.

5. Fisher, p. 203.

6. Ibid., p. 202.

7. Kennedy, p. 68.

8. Ibid., pp. 148–149, 163.

Chapter 7. Preparing for Trial

1. Noel Behn, *Lindbergh: The Crime* (New York: The Atlantic Monthly Press, 1994), p. 223.

2. Ludovic Kennedy, *The Airman and the Carpenter* (New York: Viking, 1985), p. 204.

3. Behn, p. 224.

4. Ibid.

5. Colonel Clinton L. Pagano, "The Lindbergh Kidnapping—A State Police Review," *The Triangle*, vol. 1, no. 8, March 1981, p. 12.

6. Behn, p. 226.

7. Kennedy, p. 216.

8. Behn, p. 226.

9. Kennedy, p. 212.

Chapter 8. The Trial of the Century

1. Noel Behn, *Lindbergh: The Crime* (New York: The Atlantic Monthly Press, 1994), p. 244.

2. Ibid., p. 239.

3. A. Scott Berg, *Lindbergh* (New York: G. P. Putnam's Sons, 1998), p. 309.

4. Jim Fisher, *The Lindbergh Case* (New Brunswick, N.J.: Rutgers University Press, 1987), p. 278.

5. Ibid., p. 281.

6. Ibid., p. 289.

7. *The New York Times*, January 8, 1935, p. 1.

8. Fisher, p. 315.

9. Ibid., p. 317.

10. Ibid., p. 319.

11. Ibid., p. 322.

12. Ludovic Kennedy, *The Airman and the Carpenter* (New York: Viking, 1985), p. 303.

13. Fisher, p. 327.

14. Ibid., p. 330.

15. Kennedy, p. 343.

16. Ibid., p. 344.

17. Ibid.

Chapter 9. The Appeals Process

1. Ludovic Kennedy, *The Airman and the Carpenter* (New York: Viking, 1985), p. 348.

2. Ibid., p. 349.

3. *The New York Times*, February 25, 1935, p. 6.

4. Kennedy, pp. 350–351.

5. Ibid., p. 354.

6. Ibid., p. 362.

7. Noel Behn, *Lindbergh: The Crime* (New York: The Atlantic Monthly Press, 1994), pp. 240–241 (picture caption).

8. Harold G. Hoffman, "The Crime, the Case, the Challenge," *Liberty Magazine*, February 26, 1938.

9. Ibid.

10. Kennedy, p. 395.

11. Ibid., p. 394.

Chapter 10. Case Not Closed

1. Noel Behn, *Lindbergh: The Crime* (New York: The Atlantic Monthly Press, 1994), p. 240.

2. Ludovic Kennedy, *The Airman and the Carpenter* (New York: Viking, 1985), pp. 367–368.

3. Harold G. Hoffman, "The Crime, the Case, the Challenge," *Liberty Magazine*, February 26, 1938.

4. Colonel Clinton L. Pagano, "The Lindbergh Kidnapping, A State Police Review," *The Triangle*, vol. 1, no. 8, March 1981, p. 12.

5. Behn, pp. 354–355, 376.

6. Reeve Lindbergh, "Fortress Lindbergh," *The New Yorker*, August 24 & 31, 1998, pp. 123, 126.

7. Ibid., p. 126.

8. Ibid.

★ FURTHER READING ★

Books

Behn, Noel. *Lindbergh: The Crime.* New York: The Atlantic Monthly Press, 1994.

Berg, A. Scott. *Lindbergh.* New York: G. P. Putnam's Sons, 1998.

Fisher, Jim. *The Lindbergh Case.* New Brunswick, N.J.: Rutgers University Press, 1987.

Kennedy, Ludovic. *The Airman and the Carpenter.* New York: Viking, 1985.

Lindbergh, Anne Morrow. *Hour of Gold, Hour of Lead: Diaries and Letters 1929–1932.* New York: Harcourt Brace Jovanovich, 1973.

Lindbergh, Charles A. *The Spirit of St. Louis.* New York: Charles Scribner's Sons, 1953.

Madison, Arnold. *Great Unsolved Cases.* New York: Franklin Watts, 1978.

Scaduto, Anthony. *Scapegoat: The Lonesome Death of Bruno Richard Hauptmann.* New York: G. P. Putnam's Sons, 1976.

Internet Addresses

Hunterdon County Democrat. *The Lindbergh Case: The Trial of the Century.* 1999. <http://www.lindberghtrial.com/> (May 21, 1999).

New Jersey State Police. n.d. <http://www.state.nj.us/lps/njsp/index.html> (May 21, 1999).

Public Broadcasting Service. "Lindbergh." *The American Experience.* 1999. <http://www.pbs.org/wgbh/pages/amex/lindbergh/> (May 21, 1999).

★ INDEX ★